# Ros Asquith's Teen Cookbook

## The No-Worries Guide to Cooking

First published 2009 by
A & C Black Publishers Ltd
36 Soho Square, London, W1D 3QY

www.acblack.com
www.sweetbasil.co.uk

ISBN 978-1-4081-1491-9

A CIP catalogue for this book is available from the British Library.

Design: Pumpkin House, Cambridge

This book is produced using paper that is made from wood
grown in managed, sustainable forests. It is natural, renewable
and recyclable. The logging and manufacturing processes conform
to the environmental regulations of the country of origin.

Printed and bound in Great Britain
by CPI Cox and Wyman, Reading, RG1 8EX.

# contents

# Introduction

Why are you looking at this when you could be ordering a pizza or just snacking with your head in the fridge? My guess is some 'concerned' adult foisted it on you in the hopes that you'd learn to cook better than them. Maybe they're scared you'll starve to death in college, or shack up with unsuitable mates whose fridge only ever has an empty orange plastic bag in it.

Who can blame these misguided adults? There's so much junk talked about food these days that it's surprising we're still able to chew and swallow. Bossy schools, media and the government drone on about 'youth' becoming lardy louts who'll get permanently stuck in revolving doors or need fork lift trucks to get them to infant school. Then there's the alternative nightmare: anorexics mainlining on diet sodas and alcopops, piercing themselves with Tibetan forks and refusing to eat brussels sprouts because 'plants are people too.'

So here are a few reasons to read this book instead of tossing it on the pile of other unread presents:

* It's cheaper than eating out or getting takeaways.

* It's healthier than ready meals.

* It just might make you enjoy cooking, which is handy until we can all find a pill that gives us a week's food in one go.

* It'll make you the best cook in your household/squat/ caravan/sleeping bag.

* Your mum/dad/aunty/social worker will be thrilled.

* It's hardly got any health and safety advice.

Oh, alright then, just a few things you should know…

### Five main food groups:
- *Starchy stuff*: bread, pasta, rice, donuts, potatoes
- *Fruit and vegetables* (and yes, frozen veg are fine)
- *Protein*: meat, fish, eggs, beans, peanut butter, soya
- *Dairy stuff*: milk, cheese, yogurt. (These contain calcium – it's especially good for bones so you don't get like L-shaped old bendy people you see staring at the pavement.)
- *Fat and sugar!* Yes, in moderation. They're good for energy and even brains.

It's more tasty to use fresh herbs, freshly ground black pepper, extra virgin olive oil and free range eggs and free range chicken when you can afford them or have them in your cupboard. If you're lucky enough to have a windowbox, or even a garden, it's fun to grow herbs. Remember, these recipes aren't set in stone. Have fun, experiment!

This is really all you need to know about food.

### …EXCEPT
Wash hands before cooking! Don't leave the handles of anything cooking on the hob sticking out! Make sure all fruit and vegetables are washed before using. And look up any weird words in the handy guide at the back of the book … Happy cooking!

(V) Look out for recipes marked by this sign – these are for vegetarians, or if you don't fancy cooking something with meat. You can also find all the veggie recipes in the index at the back of the book.

# Utensils Guide

**Baking tray** – flat metal sheet used for baking food such as cookies or biscuits

**Frying pan** – shallow metal pan with a handle, used for frying food

**Ladle** – deep spoon with a long handle, for serving liquids

**Long slotted spoon** – spoon with a long handle and holes/slots in its bowl, to allow liquid to drain away

**Masher** – device used for mashing food such as potatoes or fruit

**Non-stick frying pan** – pan coated with a special substance that prevents food sticking to it while cooking

**Potato ricer** – device containing lots of small holes through which cooked potatoes are forced, to break them into tiny pieces

**Ramekin** – small, individual baking dish

**Spatula** – implement that looks like a large flat spoon, which can be used to mix, spread or lift food

**Spring-form pan** – a pan used for cooking cakes, which has a detachable bottom so that the cake can be released easily

**Tablespoon** – large spoon used for serving food (the same size as three teaspoons)

**Wire rack** – metal grid on which food such as bread and cookies can be left to cool (the holes in the rack allow air to get to the bottom of the food so it will not go soggy as it cools down)

**Wok** – large metal pan (traditionally with a rounded bottom) used for Chinese cooking, such as stir-fries

# Basic Survival

OK, so you're not dangling from a crevasse in your underwear or facing a pack of ravenous wolves armed only with a biro. But you do want cheap, cosy food. Welcome to the bread, potatoes and eggs section: all you need to survive. Potatoes, surprisingly, provide 20% of Britain's vitamin C intake! They also contain protein, potassium, B vitamins. If I could have only one food in the world it would be potatoes. Boiled, baked, mashed, roasted, fried... Praise the potato!

Also here at last in this section – the simple guide to boiling an egg. Everyone agrees there's plenty of protein, vitamins and minerals in eggs. To check that an egg's fresh, put it in water. If it floats, it's stale. If it sinks, it's fresh. (This is what witch-hunters did in the olden days. If the woman sank, the good news was, she wasn't a witch. On the other hand, she drowned).

You can make your own bread too. You may recognise this recipe at present as taking your toast and scraping it. Better still, try the basic bread recipe in this bit, which is bound to impress anyone who eats it.

serves **①**

# Boiled egg & soldiers (v)

* **2 free-range eggs**
* **2 slices of bread**
* **butter**

HOW TO
BOIL AN
EGG

Part XII

### What to do

**1** Half fill a small saucepan with water and bring to the boil. Place the eggs in the water using a wooden spoon (a metal spoon gets too hot to handle) and simmer. Leave for 4 minutes to get a soft egg (set a timer to get it just right), or 5 minutes for a medium egg. If you leave the egg longer, it'll be a hard-boiled egg. You won't be able to dip the soldiers in it, but it'll be good for a picnic.

**2** While they're cooking, put some bread in the toaster or under the grill and, when it's ready, butter it. Cut the toast into strips to make the soldiers.

**3** When the eggs are cooked, remove them from the saucepan with the spoon and put them into an egg cup. Remove the top of the eggs with a spoon.

My preferred method is bashing them with the spoon and peeling off the little bits of shell...

**4** Add soldiers and get dipping!

← soldier

← egg

Wholemeal bread is miles better for you. Most people start liking it from about the age of fifteen. Before then, they'd rather die, clinging to sliced white stuff called bread but mainly made of polystyrene and toenail clippings.

# cheesy omelette (v)

*serves* **1**

* 1 tsp olive oil
* 2 large free-range eggs
* 1 tbsp chopped chives (optional)
* 50g grated cheddar cheese
* salt and black pepper

> You can buy it grated, but it's much cheaper to do it yourself. You only need to use the bigger holes in the grater, not the tiny ones that scrape your knuckles off.

## What to do

1 Mix the eggs in a small bowl, stir in the chives and add a pinch of salt and pepper.

2 Heat the oil over a medium heat in a small frying pan.

3 Pour the egg mixture into the frying pan and lower the heat.

4 Sprinkle the cheese over the middle of the omelette. When the omelette is cooked (which happens pretty quickly, so keep an eye on it) place the frying pan under the grill until the cheese melts, being careful not to put the handle under the heat. Fold one half of the omelette over the other half and serve immediately, otherwise it'll have the consistency of a bicycle tyre.

> Before eating, add a little salt and pepper (then have a taste to make sure it's salty enough).

> You can also make this without putting it under the grill, by simply stirring in the cheese along with the eggs.

serves 1

# Scrambled eggs (v)

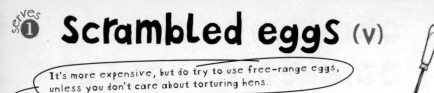

It's more expensive, but do try to use free-range eggs, unless you don't care about torturing hens.

* 4 free-range eggs
* nob of butter
* toast

* 4 tbsp milk
* salt and black pepper
* butter

## What to do

1 Whisk the eggs in a bowl with either a fork or a whisk. Add the milk and a pinch of salt and pepper and whisk again. Pour the mixture into a small saucepan, place over a medium heat, and add butter. Stir regularly, until the egg mixture is nearly cooked through.

2 Remove from heat and eat on hot buttered toast.

---

serves 2

# BLT with extra B

* 4 rashers of streaky or back bacon
* 2 slices of bread
* 2 tbsp mayonnaise

* 2 leaves of iceberg lettuce
* 4 slices of ripe tomato
* butter

## What to do

1 Grill the bacon under a medium to high heat, until crispy.

2 Spread one tablespoon of mayo on each slice of buttered bread, followed by one lettuce leaf on one slice. Arrange two slices of bacon on top of the lettuce followed by another two slices of bacon and finally the tomato and the other lettuce leaf on top of the bacon. Place the other slice of bread on top to finish off and slice diagonally.

# chicken, roast tomato & rocket ciabatta

serves
**1**

* 1 ciabatta loaf
* 1 chicken breast
* 6 cherry tomatoes, cut in half
* 1 tsp extra-virgin olive oil
* salt
* 1 tbsp balsamic vinegar
* rocket

> This is optional and pricey, but it makes bog-standard dishes taste classy and a little goes a long way.

## What to do

**1** Preheat the oven to 170°C.

**2** Place the chicken breast in the middle of a square piece of silver foil, bringing the edges of the foil up and folding them over to make a parcel. Cook in the oven for 20 minutes and then leave to cool.

**3** Place the cherry tomatoes cut side up in a roasting tin and sprinkle with salt, olive oil and balsamic vinegar (if using) and bake for 15 minutes. After 5 minutes, put the ciabatta alongside the tomatoes in the oven.

**4** Now the chicken should be cool enough to slice.

**5** Remove the ciabatta from the oven. Allow to cool for 5 minutes and then cut lengthways through the middle. Put the chicken on one half of the ciabatta, cover it with tomatoes, sprinkle with rocket, and place the rest of the ciabatta on top. Cut in half to serve.

serves
1

# Tuna mayo & Spring onion wrap

* 1 tin of tuna in brine
* 1 tbsp light mayonnaise
* 1 spring onion
* squeeze of lemon (optional)
* black pepper
* 1 carrot, peeled and grated
* 1 tortilla wrap

## What to do

1 Drain the tuna of all the brine and flake into a small bowl with a fork.

2 Cut the hairy end off the spring onion, remove the outer layer and then chop the white part up to where it turns green. Discard the green part and mix the chopped white spring onion through the tuna.

3 Mix in the mayo, a squeeze of lemon and a pinch of black pepper.

4 Place the tuna mixture towards one side of the tortilla and lay the carrot on top of the tuna. Then roll up the tortilla from the side where the mixture is placed and push the ends in to stop filling dropping out.

5 To serve, cut the tortilla in the middle, at an angle.

# croque Monsieur

This is a French ham-and-cheese toasted sandwich. If you add a poached egg on top it's called a 'Croque Madame'.

* 8 slices of bread
* 110g butter, softened
* 4 slices of ham
* 4 slices of Gruyère cheese
* 2 free-range eggs, slightly beaten
* 1 tbsp water
* salt and black pepper

Although it's perfectly tasty with cheddar.

**What to do**

1 Preheat the oven to 175°C.

2 Spread the bread with some of the softened butter, make 4 sandwiches, each with one slice of ham and one slice of cheese. Press them firmly together.

3 Beat the eggs with the water in a wide bowl, add the salt and pepper to taste, and dip the sandwiches into the egg mixture, coating all sides well.

4 Place the croque monsieurs into a very well-buttered baking pan and bake for about 10–15 minutes, turning once.

serves 2 to 4

# Garlic bruschetta

## topped with tomato, feta and basil (v)

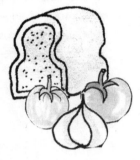

* unsliced fresh loaf of bread
* 2 garlic cloves
* 2 tbsp extra-virgin olive oil
* 6 ripe tomatoes
* 60g feta cheese
* 10g fresh basil leaves, chopped
* 1 tbsp balsamic vinegar
* salt and black pepper

**What to do**

1 Cut 4 slices of bread and toast it in the oven until brown and crisp. Cut the garlic cloves in half (to protect your fingers do not remove garlic peel). Rub the bread immediately with the cut garlic cloves, brush with olive oil and sprinkle with salt and freshly ground pepper.

2 Chop the tomatoes into bite-sized pieces, crumble the feta over the tomatoes and sprinkle with the basil leaves. Mix the olive oil and balsamic vinegar, pour over the tomatoes and toss with two spoons.

3 Top the bread with the mixture and serve.

# Pea and potato soup (v)

serves **4**

This lovely potato dish is equally delicious with leeks instead of peas.

* 2 tsp olive oil
* 1 onion, chopped
* 2 garlic cloves, crushed
* 600g Désirée potatoes, peeled, cubed
* 380g frozen peas
* 1 litre vegetable stock
* salt and black pepper, to taste
* 2 tsp single cream

## What to do

1 Heat the oil in a large saucepan over a medium heat. Add the onion and garlic and cook, stirring often, for 2–3 minutes or until the onion softens slightly. Add the potatoes, peas and stock. Increase to a high heat and bring to the boil. Reduce heat to medium and simmer, partially covered, for 10 minutes or until the potatoes are tender. Set aside for 10 minutes to cool slightly.

2 Transfer a third of the soup to a food processor and process until smooth. Place in a heatproof bowl and repeat with the remaining soup. Return all the soup to the pan and reheat over a medium-high heat, stirring for 3–4 minutes, or until hot. Taste and season with salt and pepper.

3 Ladle the soup into serving bowls. Top each with a teaspoon of cream and sprinkle with pepper.

Serve with some delicious home-made bread. See page 16.

# Basic bread recipe (v)

* ✻ 700g plain flour
* ✻ 1 packet dried yeast
* ✻ 1 tsp salt
* ✻ 400ml lukewarm water
* ✻ olive oil

## What to do

**1** Mix together the flour, dried yeast and salt in a bowl. Add the water and mix with your hands until the water has mostly disappeared.

**2** Sprinkle a little flour on a work surface and turn the dough out of the bowl onto the surface. Knead the dough by pushing the heel of your hand into the centre of the ball and pushing away from you gently, without breaking the dough. Fold the dough over, turn 45 degrees and repeat. Keep kneading until the dough feels springy when pushed in. Place the dough in a clean bowl, with a little olive oil rubbed around the inside, cover with clingfilm and put in a warm place to rise for 1½ hours or until the dough has doubled in size.

**3** Remove the dough from the bowl, and place it back onto a lightly floured surface. Knock the dough back with the heel of your hand a few times and then break it into two equal portions. Remold each portion into a large roll shape, on a baking tray with a little flour sprinkled over it, tucking the edges underneath with the edges of your hand. Cover with a clean tea towel and allow to rise again for another 1½ hours. After the dough has doubled in size again, slash 3 lines in the top of the loaves with a sharp knife.

4 Bake for 40 minutes, until the loaves are a lovely golden brown. The loaves should sound hollow when you tap the bottom. Leave to cool before cutting and serving.

If you want to try something different, add grated cheese or tomato sauce.

So that's what he meant about getting me flowers for Mother's Day...

SELF RAISING

PLAIN FLOUR

WHOLE MEAL FLOUR

# Pasta and pesto sauce (v)

**serves 2**

* 1 large basil plant, leaves only
* 25g pine kernels
* 2 cloves of garlic, crushed
* 1 tsp flaked sea salt
* 50g freshly grated Parmesan
* 150–200ml extra-virgin olive oil
* 450g pasta

> This is a delicious garlicky pasta sauce. If you buy it, the green one's made like this and the red one's made with tomatoes or peppers.

## What to do

1 Wash and dry the basil leaves.

2 Dry-fry the pine kernels over a medium heat for just 2–3 minutes, until they are slightly golden. Put in a bowl and set aside.

3 Using a food processor, drop in the basil leaves, pine kernels, garlic, salt and 150ml of olive oil and whiz to make a lovely sauce. Stir in more olive oil if the sauce is too thick. Stir in the Parmesan.

4 To serve, cook the pasta as per the instructions on the packet, drain and stir in the pesto sauce.

> To store the pesto, pour it into a jar, float a layer of olive oil on top, cover and refrigerate for up to a week.

> This is wonderful with chopped cherry tomatoes stirred through.

serves 4

# Roman-style spaghetti (v)

- 6 tbsp olive oil
- 2 cloves of garlic, crushed
- 1 red chilli, cut in half, seeds discarded, finely chopped
- 450g spaghetti
- 1 tsp salt
- 1 tbsp flat leaf parsley, chopped

**What to do**

**1** Add the salt to a pan of water and bring to the boil. Add the spaghetti and cook as per the packet instructions or until the pasta is *al dente* (cooked, but still with a very slight bite to it). Remove from the heat and drain thoroughly, then put it back in the pan.

**2** Put the olive oil, garlic and chilli in a saucepan, and cook over a medium heat. Cook until the garlic is a pale golden colour. Don't overcook the garlic as it will spoil the taste.

**3** Place the pan of pasta back on a low heat and pour the garlic and chilli oil over the pasta, add the parsley and toss with two spoons. Taste and add a little salt if necessary.

# Cottage Pie

serves **6**

* * 1 tbsp olive oil
* * 1 large onion, peeled and finely chopped
* * 1 clove garlic, peeled and crushed
* * 2 medium carrots, peeled and chopped
* * 500g beef mince
* * 1 tbsp plain flour
* * 1 tin chopped tomatoes
* * 2 tbsp tomato purée
* * 300ml stock
* * 1 tsp dried herbs de provence
* * salt and black pepper, to taste

You might be more familiar with Shepherd's pie. That's the name for this dish if you use lamb mince and it's a great veggie recipe if you substitute chickpeas for the meat.

**For the topping:**

* * 1kg white potatoes, peeled and diced
* * 75g butter
* * 4 tbsp milk
* * salt and black pepper

**What to do**

**1** Preheat the oven to 180°C.

**2** Heat the oil in a large frying pan over a medium-high heat. Add the onion, garlic and carrots and fry over a medium heat until soft. Add the mince and cook, stirring occasionally, until all the mince is brown. Add the flour, mix it in and cook for a further 3 minutes, stirring occasionally.

**3** Add the stock, tinned tomatoes, tomato purée and herbs. Season with a little salt and pepper. Simmer for 30 minutes, stirring occasionally.

**4** Whilst the mince cooks, mash the potatoes using the recipe on page 24.

**5** Check the seasoning in the mince and add a little more if necessary. Spoon the mince mixture into a casserole dish. Top with the mash, gently forking it over the mince. Dot the top with a little butter and bake for 30 minutes, until the potato topping is golden brown.

Sometimes I regret being a vegetarian

Menu
Shepherd pie
Toddler on toast
Braised banker
Politician with Parmesan

serves **1**

# Steak Sandwich
## on Spanish tomato bread

Remember, if you want rare beef, just knock the horns off a cow and chase it through a warm kitchen. Alternatively, don't overcook your steak.

* **4 ripe tomatoes, chopped in half**
* **1 garlic clove, peeled**
* **3 tbsp olive oil**
* **1 baguette**
* **3 x 200g rump steaks**
* **142 ml sour cream**
* **salt and black pepper**

### What to do

**1** Cut the baguette in half and then split each half lengthwise. Smash the garlic by laying the flat side of a knife on the clove and pressing down with the heel of your hand. Rub the garlic all over the cut side of the baguette. Next, rub the cut side of the tomatoes roughly over the baguette, chop the tomato and then scatter it all over the baguette. Drizzle with a little olive oil.

**2** Heat a griddle or frying pan over a high heat but don't allow it to smoke. Brush the steaks with oil and season with a little salt and pepper. The steaks should be sizzling when they go into the pan. Cook on each side for 4 minutes. Remove from the pan and allow to rest for a minute or two.

**3** Slice the steak thinly at an angle and lay over each piece of baguette, drizzle with sour cream and serve.

# Jacket potatoes (v)

*serves* **2**

* ✻ 2 large Désirée potatoes
* ✻ 1 tsp olive oil
* ✻ 1 tsp rock salt, flaked
* ✻ butter
* ✻ salt and black pepper

Leave out the salt for a healthier option.

**What to do**

1 Preheat the oven to 190°C.

2 Wash the potatoes thoroughly. Prick the skins a few times with a fork and rub in the olive oil and salt to give a nice crunchy skin.

3 Bake in the centre of the oven for 1½ hours, or until the skin is crisp and the centre's perfectly soft.

4 Serve straight away with a knob of butter.

Great with baked beans, grated cheese, cream cheese, sweetcorn, tuna, ham, guacamole ... or whatever you fancy!

serves 4

# Mashed potatoes (v)

* **500g potatoes**
* **50g butter**
* **30ml double cream or milk**
* **salt and black pepper, to taste**

*Maris Piper or King Edwards are good for mashing.*

## What to do

**1** Place the potatoes into a pan of cold water with a ½ teaspoon of salt. There should be enough water to cover the potatoes. Bring the water to the boil then simmer until the potatoes are tender. When you can push a knife into a potato without any resistance then the potatoes are ready. This should take about 20–25 minutes.

**2** Drain the potatoes immediately and thoroughly, and place back into the warm pan. If using a masher or whisk, add the butter and cream/milk and mash or whisk until smooth. If using a potato ricer, rice the potatoes into a bowl, add the butter and cream/milk and mix until smooth. Check the flavour and season as necessary.

← *You need a masher for this. Keep mashing until there are no lumps*

# Spicy potato wedges
## with melted cheese (v)

serves **4**

* 3 baking potatoes
* 2 tbsp olive oil
* 2 tsp paprika
* 1 tsp ground cumin
* 2 tsp crushed garlic
* ½ tsp turmeric
* 1 tsp mixed dried herbs
* 100g mature Cheddar cheese
* sea salt flakes and black pepper

**What to do**

1 Preheat the oven to 200°C.

2 Cut each potato into 8 wedges. Bring a pan of water up to boiling point and gently, using a long handled spoon, place the potatoes into the boiling water. Cook for 7 minutes, then drain in a colander and place back into the warm pan.

3 Combine all the remaining ingredients, except the cheese, in a bowl to make a spicy paste. When the potatoes are cool enough to handle, toss the potatoes in the spicy paste. Place on a baking tray, skin side down and bake for 30 minutes or until crisp and brown. Grate the cheese over the potatoes and place back in the oven for another 5 minutes.

serves **4**

# chips (v)

* **6 large potatoes**
* **3 tbsp olive oil**
* **½ tsp salt**

> Maris Piper, King Edwards or Desireé are best for chips.

### What to do

**1** Preheat oven to 200°C.

**2** Peel the potatoes and cut them into long chip shapes, the width of your finger. Wash them under the cold tap and pat dry with a paper towel. Then toss the chips in a bowl with the olive oil and salt.

**3** Put the chips on a large non-stick baking tray and spread out in a single layer. Roast for 45 minutes, turning occasionally. The chips should be golden brown outside, and soft and fluffy inside. Roast for a further 5–10 minutes if needed.

# chicken stock

serves 4

This is great for soups, stews and gravies. I like to cook rice in it, instead of plain water. It may seem like a slog to make, when you're used to crumbling a stock cube into hot water, but you get a warm glow from using up the whole chicken, just like Native Americans used to do with buffalo. Except you can't make your trousers out of a chicken.

* 1 onion, chopped
* 1 carrot, chopped
* 2 sticks of celery, chopped
* 1 chicken carcass
* 2 bay leaves
* 1 sprig of thyme
* 4 pints of cold water

**What to do**

**1** Put all the ingredients into a large saucepan and bring to the boil. Simmer for 2½ hours, regularly skimming the scum off the top of the stock.

**2** Strain through a sieve. Leave to cool and remove any fat from on top of the stock. It is now ready to use!

Refrigerate for up to 2 days or freeze for up to 3 months.

# Béchamel
## (white Sauce) (v)

serves 4

This is a basic sauce which the French call a 'roux'. Bear in mind that it was probably invented by Marquis Louis de Béchamel, who was a financier. If only bankers stuck to making sauces.

* **40g butter**
* **40g plain flour**
* **600ml milk**
* **1 bay leaf**

  Don't fret if you haven't got a bay leaf, it'll still be tasty.

* **salt and white pepper**

Use this method to make thick gravy by substituting stock for milk.

## What to do

1 Melt the butter in a saucepan. Stir in the flour until it's a smooth paste and then cook for 2 minutes, stirring as it cooks.

2 Remove from the heat and gradually stir in the milk, a little at a time. Continue until the sauce is smooth.

3 Add the bay leaf and return the sauce to the heat, stirring all the time. Bring to the boil and reduce the heat to gently simmer for 10 minutes.

4 Season with salt and white pepper to taste.

Grate cheese into this and use it for macaroni/cauliflower cheese, or lasagne.

# Feed Your Friends

Now you've mastered (or *mistressed*) the basics, you can get impressive with garlic, chocolate and duck (though preferably not all at once).

All these recipes can be converted to veggie ones by just substituting your favourite veg for fish, chicken etc (e.g. Thai Green veggie curry, bamboo shoot and noodle pancakes, tofu or soya balls with classic tomato sauce...)

Going veggie could, after all, be the big answer to global warming... just make sure you get enough protein, iron and calcium, which nuts, veg and eggs are very good for.

Also, experimenting with recipes using your own favourite foods is one way that turns you from being someone who can follow instructions into someone who can really cook. If you practise this, you can turn anything into anything. So when your fridge has half a can of baked beans, a lettuce leaf and a wedge of cheese, you may be able conjure even that into a gourmet feast. (Using a little bit of imagination and a lot of herbs).

Imagine the hordes beating a path to your door, as the fragrant whiff of Thai curry and apple crêpes wafts out to tickle their taste buds. If you're anti-social, skip this section.

# Home-baked garlic bread (v)

* ½ quantity of pizza dough recipe  See page 134
* 75g butter, softened
* 2 cloves of garlic, crushed
* 1 tsp dry oregano
* extra-virgin olive oil, to drizzle

**What to do**

1 Preheat the oven to 175°C.

2 After the pizza dough has been allowed to rise once and then knocked back, roll it out into a circle and place on a greased baking tray. Drizzle with a little olive oil and allow to rise again for another 30 minutes.

3 Bake the dough in the oven for 10 minutes.

4 Mix the softened butter with the garlic and oregano to make the garlic butter.

5 When the pizza base has come out of the oven, spread the garlic butter over the top and bake it in the oven for a further couple of minutes, until the butter is all melted. Cut up and serve.

Alternatively, drizzle all the oil and garlic onto half a baguette, and bake that.

# Mushroom Carbonara

serves **4**

* ✳ 450g penne pasta or spaghetti
* ✳ 300ml double cream
* ✳ 2 cloves of garlic, crushed
* ✳ 300g smoked pancetta, cubed
* ✳ 1 tsp olive oil
* ✳ 200g mushrooms, sliced
* ✳ 1 onion, finely sliced
* ✳ black pepper
* ✳ 100g finely grated parmesan

Or 8 rashers of smoked streaky bacon, cut into small strips.

### What to do

**1** Cook the pasta in boiling water with 1 teaspoon of salt and 1 teaspoon olive oil, as instructed on the packet.

**2** Heat the rest of the oil in a frying pan over a medium heat and fry the onions until soft. Add in the pancetta and garlic and fry for 3 minutes, stirring occasionally. Add the mushrooms and fry until cooked. Pour in the cream and cook for 5 minutes over a low heat. Season with black pepper.

**3** Drain the pasta, put it in a bowl, add the carbonara sauce and mix through.

Serve sprinkled with the Parmesan cheese

serves **4** or **8** as a snack

# Chinese duck pancakes

* 4 duck breasts, about 175g/6oz each, skin removed
* ½ tsp Chinese five spice powder
* salt and black pepper
* 5 tbsp hoisin sauce
* 2 tbsp tomato paste
* 2cm ginger, finely chopped or crushed
* 1 small clove of garlic, crushed
* 1 tsp sesame oil
* 10 Chinese pancakes
* 1 bunch spring onions
* ½ cucumber

**What to do**

1 Preheat the oven to 190° C.

2 Rub the duck breasts all over with the Chinese five spice powder and a little salt and pepper. Place them in a baking tray and bake, uncovered, for 20 minutes. Allow to cool.

*These are available from large supermarkets. If you can't find any, use mini tortillas.*

**3** Mix together the hoisin sauce, sesame oil, tomato paste, ginger and garlic. Slice the duck into bite-sized slices and cover with the sauce. Set aside in a bowl.

**4** Cut most of the green off the spring onions, cut off the hairy end and then cut into matchsticks. Cut the cucumber into matchsticks and put in a bowl with the spring onions.

**5** Warm the pancakes in the microwave for about 10 seconds. Cut the pancakes in half and put some duck, spring onion and cucumber in the pancake, then roll it up and its ready to eat.

You don't have to cut the pancakes, you could put it all in the centre of the table and let your guests tuck in.

How do you flatten a DUCK?

DUCK PAN CAKES

**33**

**serves 4**

# Thai salmon fishcakes
## with dipping sauce

*You'll wonder why you ever bought those frozen ones after trying these.*

For the salmon fillets:

* 400g salmon fillets, finely chopped
* 100g cod fillet, finely chopped
* 1 tsp Thai green curry paste
* 1 egg
* 2 tbsp Thai fish sauce
* 1 tbsp caster sugar

*Buy this from a shop or see recipe on page 38.*

* 2 tbsp cornflour
* 1 tbsp lime
* 2 tbsp coriander, finely chopped
* 1 spring onion, finely chopped
* ½ tsp salt and ½ tsp black pepper
* 2 tbsp groundnut oil

For the sweet chilli, ginger and cucumber dipping sauce:

* 4 medium chillies, seeds removed and finely chopped
* 100g caster sugar
* 100ml water
* 1 tsp grated ginger
* ¼ cucumber

*If salmon is too pricey, this'll still taste good using just cod. Or you can use hake, or haddock. Naturally, these will then be Thai cod, hake or haddock fishcakes, but maybe no one will notice.*

*Make sure you wash your hands thoroughly after touching chillies.*

Or, if you like, make a fish shape, or a wobbly blob. It's the taste that counts.

## What to do

Start with the salmon fillets...

1 Combine all the ingredients. Heat the oil in a frying pan and, using a tablespoon, place a spoon of the mix into the pan, making a nice round shape.

2 Fry for 2–3 minutes, turn over with a spatula and cook for a further 2–3 minutes. You should be able to fit 4–5 fishcakes in the frying pan. Remove onto a plate covered with a piece of kitchen roll.

Now for the dipping sauce...

3 Cut the cucumber into quarters – lengthways – and slice the middle off each piece. Then finely slice lengthways and set aside.

4 Combine the caster sugar, water and ginger, and mix until the sugar has dissolved. Mix in the chillies and then add the cucumber to complete the dipping sauce.

If you've got any dipping sauce left over after you've scoffed all your fishcakes, this is great for dipping anything else into. Nachos, carrots - it'll even make celery interesting. Just.

# Homemade meatballs

## with classic tomato sauce

For the meatballs:

* ✳ 500g extra lean minced beef
* ✳ 70g salami, chopped into small pieces
* ✳ 50g fresh white breadcrumbs

> You can buy these, but it's easy to make them by using a grater.

* ✳ 2 tbsp fresh parsley, finely chopped
* ✳ 1 clove garlic, finely chopped
* ✳ salt and black pepper
* ✳ 6 fresh basil leaves, torn
* ✳ plain flour
* ✳ 2 tbsp extra-virgin olive oil

For the rest:

* ✳ 250g linguine
* ✳ 1 clove garlic, finely chopped
* ✳ 2 small onions, finely chopped
* ✳ 2 cans of chopped tomatoes
* ✳ 4 tbsp tomato puree
* ✳ 2 tbsp oregano
* ✳ splash of white wine

This is pasta in long, thin strips — you can use spaghetti instead if you prefer.

## What to do

**1** Mix all the meatball ingredients together and shape into walnut-sized balls. Walnuts still in their shells, that is, or, if you've never seen a walnut, think table-tennis balls. Roll the meatballs in the flour to lightly coat them and then fry in hot oil until golden, turning regularly.

**2** Now prepare the tomato sauce. Sweat the chopped onion and garlic in the olive oil until soft but not brown. Add the white wine and simmer for a minute, before adding the chopped tomatoes, tomato puree and oregano. Simmer for 1 hour over a low heat, stirring every now and then. Season to taste.

**3** Add the meatballs to the tomato sauce and bake in the oven for 10 minutes at 170°C.

**4** While the meatballs are cooking, boil the pasta as per the instructions on the packet. Drain it well and ladle the meatballs and sauce on top.

If you cook it too long it goes soft and slimy. If you get it right, it's a little bit chewy, or what the Italians call 'al dente'. Delicioso!

The two things I cook best are meat balls and rhubarb crumble

Which one is this?

serves **4**

# Thai green curry

If you're short of time, buy the ready-made curry paste, which is still very good!

For the Thai green curry paste:

* 5 cloves of garlic
* 6 green chillies, seeds removed and chopped
* 2 stalks of lemongrass, outer skin removed and green part chopped off
* 3 spring onions, trimmed and chopped
* 2 tbsp coriander stalks, chopped
* 3cm ginger
* ½ onion
* 1 lime, grated zest and juice
* 1 pinch of salt
* 2 tsp ground cumin
* 1 tsp coriander seeds
* 1 tsp black peppercorns

For the rest:

* 500g skinless, boneless chicken (chopped into bite-sized pieces)
* 1 tbsp vegetable oil
* 1 tbsp palm sugar
* 1–2 stalks lemongrass
* 400ml coconut milk
* 1½ tbsp Thai fish sauce
* handful of coriander, roughly chopped
* Thai basil, roughly chopped
* red chillies, seeded and finely chopped
* 225g Thai jasmine rice

It's sometimes sold as coconut sugar or palm honey. Confused? It comes from the sap of palm tress. Climbers shin up and slash the flowers, which then drip into a bucket. Delicious, but if you can't find it, use dark brown sugar.

You can use other rice, but this is deliciously delicate.

## What to do

**1** Place all the curry paste ingredients into a food processor and whiz until smooth.

**2** Heat the oil in a heavy bottomed frying pan and brown off portions of the chicken for 3–4 minutes. Remove to a plate and continue to the next portion. When all the chicken is browned, place it back in the pan and add 2 tablespoons of the green curry paste. Stir it in to coat all the chicken.

**3** Add the coconut milk, Thai fish sauce, lime and palm sugar and simmer for 20 minutes on a very low heat, so that the sauce is barely bubbling.

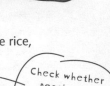

There are some tips on how to cook rice on page 150

**4** Cook the rice according to the instructions on the packet. Drain well and put the rice back in the pan, stir in the lime zest and cover with the lid to keep warm.

**5** Add the coriander and serve on the Thai jasmine rice, topped with the optional chopped Thai basil and red chillies. ←

Check whether people can handle chillies before serving these.

Chilli peppers contain capsaicinoids which have no colour, no odour and no flavour, but which still make chillies seem hot! They stimulate the mouth's pain sensors, which can produce a burning sensation, watery eyes, runny nose, and even make you sweat. Drinking water doesn't help because capsaicinoids aren't water-soluble. Milk or yogurt are soothing though.

serves 4

# Honey Teriyaki Salmon Steaks

## on Sesame Soba noodles

Teriyaki is a Japanese way of cooking. 'Teri' means 'lustre', or 'shine' and 'Yaki' means 'grill' or 'broil'. To do it really properly, you're supposed to marinade the salmon (or chicken, or beef), but this recipe is a quick way of producing something very impressive and delicious.

* 4 salmon fillets
* 8 tbsp dark soy sauce
* 2 limes, zest and juice
* 2 small chillies, seeds removed and rest finely chopped
* 4 tbsp runny honey
* 2 cloves of garlic, finely chopped
* 4cm of ginger, finely chopped
* 2 tbsp sesame oil
* 350g soba noodles
* 2 tbsp of coriander, chopped
* 2 tbsp sesame oil
* 2 tsp lime juice

These are thin Japanese noodles but any kind will do.

### What to do

1 Combine the soy sauce, ginger, garlic, lime juice and zest and the sesame oil in a dish. Coat the salmon in the mixture.

If you've got the time, leave it to marinade in the fridge for a few hours, but don't worry if not.

**2** Pan-fry the two pieces of salmon for 2 minutes each side in a hot griddle pan. Coat the salmon again in the mixture and then glaze with the honey. Put under a medium grill for 6 minutes until golden and slightly crisp.

**3** Cook and drain the noodles as specified on the packaging. Add the sesame oil, seasoning and coriander and a squeeze of lime. Place the salmon on a bed of noodles.

To serve, sprinkle with coriander.

Thanks. That was great. Now, shall we get in a pizza?

serves **6**

# Apple crêpes
## with coconut Greek yoghurt and runny honey ( V )

* 6 Granny Smith
* 2 tsp cinnamon
* 100g melted butter
* 450ml semi-skimmed milk
* 200g caster sugar
* 250g plain flour
* 2 free-range eggs
* 1 tbsp baking powder
* 1 tsp nut oil
* 1 tbsp grated coconut
* 1 pot Greek yoghurt
* runny honey

**1** Peel 5 of the apples, remove the cores and slice. Melt 50g butter over medium heat and add the apples. Sprinkle with sugar and cinnamon. Cook until the apples are soft and slightly brown. Stir occasionally to prevent sticking.

**2** Grate 1 apple on a coarse grater and place with the milk, flour, sugar, eggs, baking powder and oil in a blender and blitz until smooth.

**3** Melt the remaining butter and then lightly butter a small non-stick frying pan over a medium heat. Pour 1 ladle of batter into the frying pan, quickly lift the pan and rotate until the bottom of the pan is covered. Cook until light brown on the underside (use a spatula to lift the edge slightly to check). Using the spatula, loosen the crepe and then turn and cook the other side until light brown.

**4** Stack crêpes, with greaseproof paper and cover with a clean tea-towel.

**5** To serve, fill each crêpe with the apple, yoghurt and a drizzle of the honey, fold in the sides and roll to make a parcel.

You want **SIX** apples?! I'm not **made** of money! Apples don't grow on **trees** ... whoops

# Gooey double chocolate and pecan brownies (v)

makes **25**

* 475g dark chocolate with over 50% cocoa solids
* 375g unsalted butter
* 220g plain flour
* 6 large free-range eggs
* 500g caster sugar
* 2 tsp vanilla extract
* ½ tsp salt
* 100g pecan nuts, roughly chopped

**What to do**

1 Preheat an oven to 175°C.

2 Line a square baking tray with silver foil.

3 Chop 100g of the chocolate into large chunks and mix in the pecans. Set aside. Break the rest of the chocolate into pieces, cut the butter into chunks and place in a microwavable bowl. Microwave for 2 minutes and 10 seconds. Alternatively, melt the chocolate in a bowl over a pan of hot water.

4 Mix the eggs, sugar and vanilla extract in a separate large bowl and then mix into the chocolate until well combined. Add the flour and salt and swiftly mix to remove lumps of flour. Add the chopped chocolate and pecans and transfer to the baking tray. Bake for 30 minutes.

5 Leave to cool totally before removing from the tray. Slice into squares.

# Be Nice to Your Family

Whether you live with just one person or four generations, you may find you never meet over a meal.

*Somebody's* got to keep the family together... It could be you! This section's full of comforting meals that you'd love to have had as a small kid (if your mum hadn't been so busy making you eat sprouts, which taste like the fart of a frog, although don't tell anyone I said so).

Here you can give papaya to your papa or granda to your granny. It even includes good old-fashioned bread and butter pudding ('Brioche and butter pudding', to make it sound fancy) and toad in the hole. Is it only the British who have food names like this? At least I haven't included spotted dick, one must draw the line somewhere.

If you live in a perfectly functional family (at least one sober adult in the home), give them a big treat of breakfast in bed and thank your lucky stars you've got someone to butter up.

# Granola (v)

serves **6**

By now you've probably heard that lots of ready-made breakfast cereals have about as much nutritional value as a packet of crisps. So, why not actually just have a packet of crisps? Because they won't give you as much energy as fabulous, tasty granola!

* 300g rolled oats
* 75g flaked almonds
* 50g sunflower seeds
* 50g pumpkin seeds
* ¼ tsp salt
* 1 tsp ground cinnamon
* 2 tbsp unsalted butter, melted

Let's be honest, all this fruit, flake and nut stuff is optional. You can add different nuts, honey, chocolate flakes, banana slices – anything you fancy.

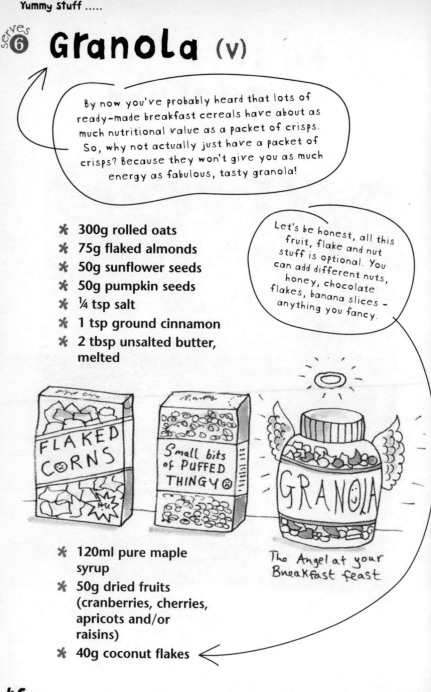

The Angel at your Breakfast feast

* 120ml pure maple syrup
* 50g dried fruits (cranberries, cherries, apricots and/or raisins)
* 40g coconut flakes

**What to do**

1 Grease a regular baking tray.

2 Combine the oats, almonds, seeds and coconut, and set aside.

3 In a small saucepan, over a medium heat combine the syrup, butter and cinnamon. Bring the mixture to a simmer and cook, for 1 minute, stirring continuously.

4 Remove from the heat and pour over the oat mixture until it is coated.

5 Lay the oats over the bottom of the baking tray and bake at 140°C for 30–35 minutes, or until golden brown. Stir the mixture every 10 minutes during this time.

6 Remove the granola from the oven and mix in the dried fruits. Leave to cool, stirring occasionally. Store in an airtight container.

This will keep in the fridge for several weeks. It's great as a snack food with no extra liquid, or you can eat it like cereal with milk, yoghurt or fruit juice. I even like it with hot water.

# makes 12 chocolate nut muffins (v)

* 125g plain chocolate
* 100g shelled brazil nuts, roughly chopped
* 225g self-raising flour
* 1 tsp baking powder
* 55g dark brown soft sugar
* 225ml milk
* 60ml vegetable oil
* 1 tsp vanilla essence
* 1 large free-range egg

You could use a different kind of nut – walnuts would be nice too!

## What to do

1 Preheat the oven to 220°C.

2 Place muffin paper cases in a muffin tin, or regular baking tray.

3 Fill a saucepan ⅓ full with water and heat to just below simmering. Place the chocolate in a bowl, which should fit on the top of the pan but not touch the water. Or you can cut up the chocolate and just put it in the microwave for 1 minute.

**4** Sift the flour. Then beat the flour and all the remaining ingredients, gently into the chocolate. Don't worry if there are still lumps, the less you work the mixture the lighter the muffin.

**5** Spoon the mixture into the paper cases and bake in the preheated oven for 15 minutes. The muffins should be well risen and firm to the touch. Transfer the muffins out of the tin onto a wire rack to cool.

Eat warm or cold. Decorate with flaked almonds, a raspberry or even some sweets.

# American pancakes

## with banana and maple syrup (v)

These are those little round fat pancakes, like Scotch pancakes. Well, they are Scotch pancakes really, only for some reason the Scots like to eat them with butter and honey (so do I) whereas the Americans go for syrups and fruit.

* 270g plain flour
* 2 tsp baking powder
* 1 tsp salt
* 4 tbsp caster sugar
* 280ml semi skimmed milk
* 2 large free-range eggs, lightly beaten
* 4 tbsp melted butter
* 2 bananas
* 6 tbsp maple syrup

**What to do**

1 Sift the flour, baking powder, caster sugar and salt into a large bowl. Lightly whisk together the milk and eggs. Make a well in the centre of the flour and gently pour in half the milk and egg mixture. Whisk in the centre, gradually pulling in more of the flour into the mix and adding more of the milk mixture as you go. Keep mixing until all the lumps have gone. Then mix in the melted butter.

**2** Heat a non-stick frying pan over a medium heat. Add a heaped teaspoon of butter and when it's melted pour in a ladle of the batter at a time. When they start to bubble on the top, turn the pancakes over using a spatula and cook until they are golden and puffed up.

> I can normally fit two or three pancakes in the pan at a time.

**3** Remove the pancakes to a plate and just keep piling them up. If you need to, you can put the plate of pancakes in a very low-heat oven to keep them warm.

**4** Serve with maple or golden syrup and sliced banana.

> Or... strawberries, raspberries, blueberries, or blackberries or even delicious vanilla ice cream. Or butter and honey. Or Marmite. Why not? I have personally been known to put cream cheese on these, although foodies say you should only do that to a bagel.

Take your pick!

# Porridge with papaya (v)

* 300g oats
* 8 cups water or milk
* salt, to taste
* honey, to taste
* 2 papayas
* a little extra milk

**What to do**

1 Put the oats in a saucepan. Then add milk or water and stir well, so there are no lumps. Bring to the boil and then simmer for 10–15 minutes, stirring regularly, so that the porridge does not stick to the saucepan and burn.

2 Peel and slice the papaya. When the porridge has thickened, pour onto a plate, lay the papaya on top in a circle and serve drizzled with honey.

# Mustard and tarragon chicken

serves 4

* 4 chicken breasts
* 100ml Dijon mustard
* 150ml extra-virgin olive oil
* 1 tbsp dried tarragon leaves
* ½ tsp black pepper

**What to do**

1 Preheat the oven to 190°C.

2 Place the chicken breasts in an oven-proof dish, in a single layer. In a bowl, whisk together the mustard, olive oil, tarragon and pepper, pour it over the chicken breasts and turn the breasts over in the sauce.

3 Bake the chicken breasts in the oven for 20 minutes. Pierce the chicken in the thickest part of the breast, if the juice runs clear, the chicken is cooked. If the juice isn't clear, place the chicken back in the oven for 5 minutes.

serves 4

# Sausage and mash with onion gravy

* 12 Cumberland or pork sausages

For the gravy:

* 3 large onions, thinly sliced
* 500ml chicken or beef stock
* 75g butter
* 2 tsp French mustard
* salt and black pepper

You can make a perfectly nice gravy much quicker, using basic gravy granules and water. But it won't be as mouth-watering as this one.

For the mash:

* 1kg Maris Piper potatoes, peeled and cut into pieces
* 150ml milk
* 50ml double cream
* 1 tbsp of butter

If you're taking the trouble to get a really tasty gravy, which takes an hour, then start with that, then put the spuds on, then start cooking the sausages when the potatoes are nearly done. That way the whole thing takes an hour. If you can't multi-task, it will take longer.

**What to do**

For the gravy:

**1** Place a heavy pan on a medium heat and melt the butter, cook the onion in the butter for 20 minutes, stirring frequently until the onions are softened. If you don't stir, they'll stick to the pan and burn. After 20 minutes, lower the heat to the lowest setting and cook until the onions are brown. This takes a long time, so be prepared to wait – this should take about an hour in total. The long cooking time gives the gravy a great taste and colour.

**2** Add the stock and mustard. Then bring the gravy up to a simmer, stirring frequently.

**3** Check the seasoning and add pinch of salt and pepper to taste.

For the mash:

**1** Bring half a pan of water to the boil and cook the potatoes for 20 minutes. The potatoes are cooked when you can pierce them with a knife and the potato drops off.

**2** When cooked, drain the potatoes in a colander and put them back in the saucepan. Add the butter, milk and double cream and mash together until smooth.

**3** Season with salt and pepper and put the lid back on the saucepan to keep them warm.

For the sausages:

**1** Fry the sausages in a little oil in a frying pan over a medium heat for about 10 minutes until cooked, turning frequently.

**2** To serve place the mashed potatoes in the centre of the plates, lean 3 sausages on the mashed potatoes and serve with the onion gravy poured over the top. This way it looks as mouth-watering as it tastes...

# Spaghetti Bolognese

* 1kg lean minced beef
* 120g bacon, chopped
* 2 tbsp olive oil
* 2 cloves of garlic
* 2 small onions, finely chopped
* 3 carrots, chopped
* 2 tbsp thyme, finely chopped
* 2 bay leaves
* 2 cans of chopped tomatoes
* 240ml red wine
* 250ml beef stock, made from a stock cube
* 4 tbsp tomato puree
* salt and black pepper
* 20g fresh basil to garnish, chopped
* 20g flat leaf parsley, chopped
* 600g spaghetti
* 200g freshly grated Parmesan cheese

## What to do

1 Heat the oil in a medium saucepan and gently fry the onions, bacon, carrot and garlic for 5 minutes, stirring regularly. Add the mince and cook for 5 minutes until brown, stirring occasionally.

**2** Add the wine, chopped tomatoes, stock, thyme and tomato puree. Bring to the boil. Add the bay leaf and season with a good pinch of salt and pepper, reduce the heat and simmer for 30 minutes. Add the basil and parsley, stir and cook for a further 5 minutes.

**3** Bring 2 pints of water to boiling point, add ½ tablespoon of salt to the water. Then add the spaghetti to the pan, pushing it against the base of the pan until it is all in the water. Stir once and simmer for 10 minutes. Check the pasta by tasting it, it should be soft but also slightly firm to the bite. Place the drained spaghetti on a plate and spoon the Bolognese sauce on top.

Serve with a sprinkling of Parmesan cheese.

serves 4

# chicken
# Caesar Salad
## with chunky croutons

* 4 boneless chicken breasts
* 2 large Cos or Romaine lettuce, bottoms removed and leaves separated and washed.
* 6 slices of thick-sliced crusty bread
* 4 tbsp olive oil
* 2 tsp herbs de provence
* 2 cloves of garlic
* 4 anchovy fillets
* 12 tbsp light mayonnaise
* 2 tbsp white wine vinegar
* block of Parmesan, for shaving
* sea salt and black pepper

You can get tinned anchovy fillets. Miss these out if you don't like the taste!

**What to do**

1 Heat the oven to 200°C.

2 Cut the bread into large chunks with a bread knife. Spread over a large baking tray and sprinkle over 2 tablespoons of olive oil. Toss the oil into the bread and season with a little sea salt. Bake for 10 minutes, turning the croutons a few times during cooking till they're golden brown and crispy.

**3** Rub the chicken breasts with the remaining oil and herbs de provence, and season with a little salt and pepper. Lay the chicken in a square piece of silver foil, big enough to fold both sides up to the top, above the chicken and fold over the chicken, sealing all the way around to make a parcel. This should seal the chicken in. Place in the oven and cook for 20 minutes more. Check if it's cooked by poking the tip of a sharp knife into the thickest part – if cooked, the juices should run clear with no pinkness.

**4** Peel off the skin of the garlic and crush with a garlic crusher or dice with a sharp knife. Mix in the anchovies (if using) with a fork, mashing against the side of the bowl. Mix in the mayonnaise, vinegar and a grating of cheese to taste.

**5** Shave the cheese with a peeler. Tear lettuce into large pieces and put both in a large bowl. Pull the chicken into bite-size strips and scatter half over the leaves, along with half of the croutons. Add most of the dressing and toss with your fingers. Scatter the rest of the chicken and croutons, then drizzle with the remaining dressing.

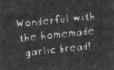

Wonderful with the homemade garlic bread!

Sprinkle the Parmesan on top and serve straight away.

You can use peppers or cherry tomatoes with this and most recipes don't use anchovies but Jamie Oliver says you should. I like to mix in a bit of creme fraiche too, if it's in the fridge.

Yummy stuff .....

serves
6

# Vegetable Lasagne

## with baby leaf and cherry tomato salad (v)

Follow the recipe for béchamel on page 28.

For the lasagne:

* 2 boxes of lasagne sheets
* 2 small onions, chopped
* 2 tbsp olive oil
* 2 aubergines, cubed
* 4 medium courgettes, cubed
* 2 yellow peppers, seeds removed and cubed
* 300g button mushrooms, quartered
* 240g spinach, rinsed and chopped
* 2 cloves of garlic
* ½ tsp of dried oregano
* 2 tins of chopped tomatoes
* 240g ricotta cheese
* 240g mozzarella, sliced
* salt and black pepper
* 2 quantities of béchamel sauce
* 100g Cheddar cheese

For the salad:

* baby leaf salad
* 20 cherry tomatoes

For the vinaigrette:

* 2 tbsp white wine vinegar
* 2 tsp mild mustard
* small pinch of sugar
* 6 tbsp extra-virgin olive oil

Wholegrain or Dijon are good.

Everyone always tells you to do this with aubergines, because it's supposed to make them less bitter and stop them absorbing too much oil. If you're in a hurry, you can skip it. They taste fine without.

**What to do**

1 Preheat the oven to 175°C.

2 Place the cubes of aubergine in a colander, sprinkle with salt and leave to drain for 30 minutes. Blot with kitchen towel.

3 Place the prepared courgettes, aubergines, peppers and mushrooms in a baking tray, toss in 1 tablespoon of olive oil, season with salt and pepper, and then roast for 30 minutes on a high shelf in the oven.

2 Heat 1 tablespoon of olive oil in a frying pan and sauté the onions and garlic, until the onions are soft. Add the spinach and cook for a further 2 minutes, stirring. Add the oregano and tinned tomatoes, season with a good pinch of salt and pepper, and cook over a low heat for 40 minutes. Add the spinach and simmer for a further 2 minutes. Now add the roasted vegetables and stir.

3 When the béchamel has been made, add the Cheddar and stir until the cheddar cheese is melted, then add the ricotta cheese and remove from the heat.

4 Now layer your lasagne with half of the roasted vegetable mix, followed by a layer of lasagne sheets, followed by half of the mozzarella and finally the cheese sauce. Repeat the process and finally sprinkle with Parmesan and bake for 30 minutes.

5 Whisk the vinaigrette ingredients together. Slice the cherry tomatoes in half and toss into the salad leaves. Just before serving, dress with a tablespoon of vinaigrette and toss.

serves 4

# Fabulous fish pie

This is a pretty gourmet version – of course, you can always just choose one kind of fish to keep it simpler and cheaper.

* 1kg potatoes
* 50g butter
* 2 free-range eggs, hard boiled
* 40g butter
* 40g flour
* 500ml milk
* 150g medium Cheddar cheese
* 1 tbsp flat leaf parsley, chopped
* 200g salmon fillets, skinned and boned
* 300g haddock or coley fillets, skinned and boned
* 200g undyed smoked haddock fillets, skinned and boned
* salt and black pepper

"Undyed?" I hear you ask. Sorry, but most smoked haddock is made with modern machinery instead of a proper fire, so it's dyed with yellow food colour to give it that traditional look.

## What to do

1 Boil the potatoes in salted water until soft enough, so that when pierced with a knife they fall off back into the water. Mash with the butter and a little salt and pepper.

2 Cut the fish into pieces that will fit into a saucepan and place them in the saucepan with 500ml milk. Then heat the fish and milk, stirring occasionally, until the milk starts to boil. At this point, turn the heat off, cover with a lid and leave for 10 minutes. When cooked, remove the fish from the pan and strain the milk to make the sauce with later.

**3** Flake the fish into a large well-buttered ovenproof dish. Chop the eggs and mix well with the fish.

This means scraping it into flakes with a fork.

**4** Melt the butter in a small saucepan and add the flour, stirring constantly for 2 minutes. Slowly add 250ml of the milk used to poach the fish, stirring constantly. Bring up to simmering point. Add the parsley, and season with salt and pepper. Mix the sauce in with the fish and egg mixture.

**5** Spread mashed potato on top of the pie and then the grated cheese. Bake in the oven for 25 minutes, or until golden.

Serve with garden peas.

# Roast chicken with garlic and rosemary

*In most cookbooks, this would be called 'oven roasted' chicken. I'm not sure why. After all, where else would you roast a chicken?*

serves **6** to **8**

* 1 large chicken
* 1 clove of garlic, peeled and cut in half
* 1 lemon, cut in half
* 2 sprigs of rosemary
* 1 tbsp olive oil
* salt and black pepper

*Use more garlic, if you like. I often use 3 or 4 cloves.*

*You can use dried, but fresh is tastier.*

**What to do**

**1** Preheat the oven to 230°C.

**2** Wash the chicken in cold water and pat dry with kitchen paper – don't use a teatowel! Rub the chicken all over with the garlic and set the garlic aside. Place the chicken in a baking tray and squeeze the lemon inside and out.

**3** Finely chop 1 sprig of rosemary and rub it all over the chicken skin, along with the olive oil, salt and pepper. Place the other sprig of rosemary in the inside of the chicken along with the garlic. Cook the chicken on the high heat for the first 15 minutes, then turn the temperature down to 190°C and cook for a further 1 hour and 10 minutes, basting a couple of times whilst cooking.

**4** When cooked, place the chicken onto a warmed serving
dish, cover with foil and allow it to rest for 10 minutes
before carving.

This chicken can be served with rice and salad,
but is delicious with roast potatoes, bread sauce,
and loads of gravy. Madke gravy with the juices
from the chicken and a bit of flour – like the
béchamel sauce on page 28 but without the milk.
Cook some carrots by boiling for 10 minutes in
butter and brown sugar with a teeny bit of water
and some peas.

That chicken doesn't look too good

If it's looks you're after, cook a peacock

# Lamb Tajine

serves **6**

This is a delicious Moroccan dish, so called because it's cooked in a tajine. But I reckon it tastes just as good in a casserole dish. Ask a Moroccan chef if you don't believe me.

* 1kg lamb shoulder, cut into 5cm chunks
* 1 tbsp ground ginger
* ½ tsp black pepper
* 1 tbsp ground cinnamon
* ½ tbsp ground turmeric
* 1½ tbsp sweet smoked paprika
* 1 tsp cayenne pepper
* 1 tbsp olive oil
* 3 tbsp groundnut oil
* 2 onions, finely chopped
* 3 garlic cloves, crushed
* 50g ready-to-eat apricots, cut in half
* 50g flaked almonds
* 1 tbsp clear honey
* 400ml tomato juice
* 400ml lamb stock
* 400g chopped tomatoes
* 2 tbsp fresh coriander, chopped
* 1 tbsp fresh flat leaf parsley, chopped

You can buy these in a packet.

**What to do**

1 Preheat the oven to 140°C.

2 Mix the pepper, ginger, cinnamon, turmeric, paprika and cayenne pepper in a bowl. Put half the mix in a large bowl and coat the lamb pieces, then set aside, covered with cling film.

**3** Heat one tablespoon of olive oil and one tablespoon of groundnut oil in a large flame-proof casserole dish over a medium heat. Evenly brown batches of lamb, removing each batch from the pan to a dish, and repeat until all of the lamb has been cooked.

**4** Add the remaining olive and groundnut oil to the casserole dish and stir in the onion. Add the rest of the spice mix and cook for 5 minutes, stirring occasionally. Add in the garlic and continue to cook for 3 minutes. The onions should be soft but not brown.

**5** Add the lamb back into the casserole dish with the apricots, almonds, honey, tomato juice, chopped tomatoes and lamb stock. Bring to the boil, then transfer it to the oven and cook for 1½ hours. The lamb should be completely tender (cook for a further 20 minutes if not tender). 10 minutes from the end of cooking mix add in the the coriander and parsley.

> The longer this cooks, the better it is. And, as long as you brown the lamb first, you can more or less toss all the ingredients in at once.

**6** Serve with spiced couscous.

> See the recipe on the next page.

# Spiced couscous (v)

serves 6

* 1 tbsp olive oil
* 2 cloves of garlic, finely chopped
* 1 tsp ginger, finely diced
* 1 onion, finely diced
* 1 tsp cumin seeds
* 1½ tsp fennel seeds
* 1½ coriander seeds
* ½ small dried chilli, chopped (make sure you wash your hands after chopping)
* a pinch of turmeric
* 1 lemon, zest and juice
* 1 tbsp red wine vinegar
* 1 tsp sugar
* 380g uncooked couscous
* 535ml boiling water and stock cube
* 1 tbsp finely chopped coriander, leaves and stems to garnish

**What to do**

1 Heat the oil over a medium heat in a deep pan with a thick bottom, add the butter and slowly fry the onions until soft. Stir occasionally. With a pestle and mortar (or, if pushed, put the spices in a teatowel and smash them with a rolling pin!) crush the cumin, fennel, coriander seeds and chilli. Add the crushed spices, ginger and garlic to the onions and fry off for 3 minutes, stirring. Add the vinegar, lemon and sugar and bubble for a further 5 minutes. Add the couscous and mix through the mixture in the pan.

2 Add the water to the couscous and stir, cook over a low heat for 5 minutes (do not stir any more). Turn off the heat and cover with a teatowel for 10 minutes. Serve hot or cold.

# Dauphinoise potatoes (v)

Serves 4 to 6

You can use any old potato, but these are ideal.

* 25g butter, softened
* 1kg King Edward or Désirée potatoes
* 2–4 cloves of garlic, crushed
* 300ml double cream
* ½ onion, finely chopped
* 300ml milk
* 25g Parmesan cheese
* salt and black pepper

## What to do

1 Preheat the oven to 170°C.

2 Brush the sides of a casserole dish with the butter.

3 Peel and thinly slice the potatoes, rinse with cold water and pat dry with kitchen paper. Layer the potatoes in the dish, slightly overlapping the slices. When finished, sprinkle a little of the crushed garlic, onion, salt and pepper over the potatoes. Mix the milk and cream and pour a quarter of the mixture over the first layer.

4 Layer the rest of the potatoes, in the same manner, making sure garlic, onion, seasoning and cream mixture are added after each layer. Layer until all the potatoes are used up. Then pour the rest of the cream over the top and sprinkle with the Parmesan.

5 Place the potatoes in the oven and cook for 1 hour, or until the top is golden and the potatoes are tender when pierced. Rest for 5 minutes before serving.

Not you – the potatoes! Although you deserve a rest after all that slicing and layering.

**69**

# Toad in the hole
## with onion gravy

Nothing amphibian about this. Just sausages in Yorkshire pud...

**For the gravy:**

* 2 red onions
* 2 tbsp olive oil
* 2 knobs of butter
* 2 tbsp plain flour
* 550ml chicken stock
* 2 tsp Marmite
* 2 tsp dried thyme
* salt and black pepper, to taste

**For the rest:**

* 4 free-range eggs
* 250g plain flour
* 300ml milk mixed with 300ml cold water
* 2 tbsp wholegrain mustard
* salt and black pepper
* 8 fat, herby pork sausages
* 200g thinly sliced prosciutto, pancetta, Serrano ham or thin streaky bacon
* 6 tbsp vegetable oil

**What to do**

1 Preheat the oven to 220°C.

2 Sift the flour into a large bowl with the salt and pepper. Make a hole in the middle of the flour and add the eggs into the hole. Gradually mix the eggs, using a hand whisk, bringing in a little of the flour at a time and adding a little milk at a time. Work the whisk further out, incorporating more and more of the flour as you work. When the batter is smooth, with no lumps, rest for 15 minutes. The batter should be like double cream.

**3** While the batter's resting, fry the sausages until golden brown all over. Remove the sausages to a plate and pour the oil into a deep roasting tin, big enough to hold the sausages with a gap in between. Put the roasting tin in the oven and heat until the oil is smoking. Then remove the roasting tin from the oven and pour in the batter, which will sizzle softly in the fat.

**4** Arrange the sausages in the batter and transfer the tin back into the oven and bake for 25–30 minutes, until puffed and golden.

**5** Whilst the toad in the hole is in the oven, slice the onions. Heat the olive oil and butter over a low heat, add the onions and fry for 8 minutes or until the onions are soft and transparent. Add the flour and stir well. Let the flour brown a little in colour.

**6** Finally, add the stock gradually, stirring constantly. Add the Marmite and thyme. Season, bring to the boil and simmer for 20 minutes until the gravy is thickened. Remove the toad in the hole from the oven. Cut in two and place on plates. Pour over gravy and enjoy!

serves **4**

# Lemon and almond torte (v)

* 450g unsalted butter, softened
* 550g caster sugar
* 450g coarsely ground almonds
* 2 tsp pure vanilla extract
* 6 free-range eggs
* finely grated zest of 4 lemons
* juice of 1 lemon
* 300g finely ground polenta (cornmeal)
* 1½ tsp baking powder
* ¼ tsp salt
* icing sugar, for dusting
* 50g slivered almonds
* fresh berries for garnish
* thick double cream

> What is a torte? A cake, really, but made with lots of eggs and usually using grated nuts or breadcrumbs (but, in this case, polenta) instead of flour.

## What to do

1 Preheat the oven to 170°C.

2 Rub some butter on the base and sides of a straight-sided cake pan. Sprinkle flour on the base of the pan and tap it around to cover all of the butter. A spring-form pan (one with a detachable bottom and a clamp on its side that easily releases the cake) works well for this.

**3** Beat the butter and sugar together with an electric mixer until pale and light. Stir in the ground almonds and vanilla.

**4** Beat in the eggs, one at a time then fold in the lemon zest and lemon juice. Next, mix together the polenta, baking powder and salt, and add them to the mixture.

**5** Spoon into pan and bake in the preheated oven for 45–50 minutes, or until set (the cake should just begin to come away from the sides of the pan and will be deep brown on top).

**6** Cool on a rack for 20 minutes, then gently remove to a serving plate, right-side up.

**7** Sprinkle the top with the slivered almonds.

to serves 4 6

# Apple and cinnamon crumble (v)

You can use other cooking apples, too.

* ✳ 750g medium to large Bramley apples
* ✳ 4 tbsp caster sugar, or Demerara sugar
* ✳ ¼ tsp ground cinnamon
* ✳ 1 tbsp lemon juice
* ✳ 115g plain flour
* ✳ 60g rolled oats
* ✳ 110g butter, cold from fridge

**What to do**

1 Preheat the oven to 190°C.

2 Peel and cut the apples into quarters, also cutting out the core from the apples. Slice them thickly and put them into a large saucepan. Add the sugar, as well as the cinnamon, lemon and 3 tablespoons water. Cover and cook for 10 minutes over a low heat, shaking the pan occasionally until the apple pieces are soft. Taste for sweetness, adding a little extra sugar, if needed.

**3** Butter a shallow baking dish and spread the apple pieces over the bottom of the dish. Leave the apple to cool.

**4** To make the crumble topping, place the flour and butter into a mixing bowl, and rub together with your fingers until the mixture resembles coarse breadcrumbs. Stir in the oats and sugar.

**5** Spread the crumble mixture evenly over the apples and press down gently to level the top. Bake for 45 minutes, or until golden and crisp. The fruit juices should be bubbling along the sides of the dish.

Serve with cream, vanilla ice cream (or any flavour you fancy) or custard.

Custard: A detestable substance produced by a malevolent conspiracy of the hen, the cow, and the cook

AMBROSE
BIERCE
1842-
1914

serves
8

# Brioche and butter pudding

A delumptious variation of traditional bread and butter pud...

* 6 chocolate-chip brioche rolls
* 50g butter, softened
* 3 tsp soft brown sugar
* 3 tbsp caster sugar
* 2 medium free-range eggs
* 2 egg yolks
* 250ml double cream
* 250ml milk
* 150g sultanas
* 1 tbsp smooth orange marmalade
* 1 vanilla pod seeds

**What to do**

1 Preheat the oven to 180°C.

2 Slice the brioche rolls lengthways and butter them. Then grease the sides of a medium ovenproof dish with butter and arrange the rolls in the dish, overlapping them. Melt the marmalade over a low heat, brush it over the brioche and then sprinkle sultanas on top.

Collect the seeds by splitting the vanilla pod lengthways and scraping them out with a knife.

3 Place the eggs, egg yolks, caster sugar and brown sugar in a bowl, and whisk until light and fluffy. Add the milk, cream and vanilla seeds, whisk well and pour over the brioche. Leave to stand for 30 minutes. Then bake for a further 30–40 minutes, in the centre of the oven, until the top is golden brown and softly set.

Remove from the oven and rest for 5 minutes before serving. Serve with thick cream, berries and a dusting of caster sugar.

# Party

## Party worries:

1 Will anyone come?
2 Will everyone come including gatecashers and the crack addicts over the road?
3 Will they have a good time?
4 Will YOU have a good time? Or will your true love get off with someone else under your nose? Or because of your nose?

You can minimise these worries by cooking up a storm so that at least you're in control of the food. What's more, a couple of chicken satay skewers washed down with a handful of cheese and ham puffs will steady your pre-party nerves like nothing else. Get one good friend to help you so that if nobody turns up you can have a midnight feast together. (NB Avoid Worry number 2 by NOT putting your party on Facebook).

If it's a Summer party, and you've got a yard, then the BBQ recipes are brilliant, because you can fuss about with skewers and charcoal instead of having to think of things to say. And if you burn stuff, that's OK, with a BBQ it's what people expect.

Alternatively, practise all this for your parents' party and it might lead to you getting to cater for their friends. Let's be honest, your own friends are more likely to be interested in other things at parties.

# Seven Layer Mexican dip (v)

Ripe avocados should feel soft to the squeeze but not squidgy!

This dip is layers of beans, guacamole, onion, sour cream, cheese, salsa and tomato.

* 1 tin of refried beans
* 3 ripe avocados
* 1 clove of garlic
* 2 tbsp chopped onion
* 1 tsp lime juice
* 4 spring onions
* 240ml sour cream
* 250g medium Cheddar cheese, grated
* 1 jar of salsa
* 5 tomatoes
* salt and black pepper

You can get these in the Mexican sections of supermarkets. They're pinto beans, first boiled, then mashed and fried with onion, garlic and spices.

## What to do

1 Cover the bottom of a large bowl with the refried beans.

2 Cut the avocado in half and twist to pull apart, remove the stone and scoop out the inside.

Try making refried beans yourself using any old beans (OK, not runner beans) but if they're dried, remember to soak them overnight before boiling. I'm thinking of trying it with a tin of baked beans. Why not?

3 To make the guacamole layer, crush the garlic and put it in the food processor with the onion, avocados, lime juice, 1 teaspoon of salsa and tomatoes. Whiz it all together. Add a pinch of salt and then spread the guacamole over the top of the refried beans.

**4** Cut the top part of the green spring onions and throw them away. Then snip the green part of the spring onions with scissors, positioning them over the guacamole layer so small pieces scatter all over.

**5** Spread sour cream over the guacamole and onion, then cover the sour cream with the grated Cheddar until no sour cream is showing.

**6** Finally, blob the salsa over the cheese, using a spoon to spread it out evenly. Chop the tomatoes into bite-size pieces and sprinkle all over the top of the dip.

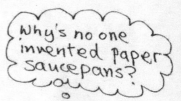

You've finished! So now just dip your nachos in deep, it's a great shared starter or a meal in itself!

Why's no one invented paper saucepans?

**79**

serves 4

# cheese and ham puffs

- **250g Emmental cheese, thinly sliced**
- **2 blocks of puff pastry**
- **2 x 80g packets of prosciutto**
- **1 free-range egg**

Prosciutto is a thin Italian ham.

**What to do**

**1** Preheat the oven to 190°C.

**2** Roll out one block of pastry to 3 cm thick and place on a flat baking tray. Cover the pastry with a layer of prosciutto, and then cover the prosciutto with the cheese. Then add another layer of the prosciutto.

**3** Roll out the other block of pastry and place over the prosciutto. Whisk up the egg and brush the pastry all over with it. Bake for 30 minutes, or until the pastry has puffed right up and is crispy. When taken out of the oven, leave for 10 minutes.

**4** Cut into 10 cm squares and enjoy.

How do we make Party nibbles?
Cut a quiche into 50 pieces

# Sesame, mustard and honey cocktail sausages

serves 4

* 30 cocktail sausages
* 3 tbsp runny honey
* 1 tsp Dijon mustard
* 2 tbsp sesame seeds

Cocktail sausages are a familiar sight at parties. They always get eaten, but do they get enjoyed? With mustard, honey and nutty sesame, they will!

**What to do**

1 Preheat the oven to 180°C.

2 Place the sausages in a single layer in a roasting tin in the oven and cook for 15–20 minutes, or until golden brown and cooked through. Turn occasionally.

3 Mix together, in a bowl, the mustard, honey and sesame seeds. Remove the sausages from the oven and pour the honey mixture over them, stirring to completely coat them with the mixture.

4 Cook for another 6–8 minutes until the sausages are bubbling and cooked, turning once.

Make sure you watch towards the end of cooking, as the sausages can burn easily.

# serves 2 chicken satay

## with spicy peanut dip

For the dip:

* 2 tbsp roasted peanuts
* 1 lemongrass stalk
* 1 shallot
* 1 clove of garlic
* 1 cm ginger
* ½ tsp turmeric
* ½ tbsp sunflower oil
* ½ tbsp brown sugar
* ½ tsp fish sauce
* ½ red chilli, finely chopped
* juice of ½ lime
* 2 tbsp water

Satay is a shish kebab-style dish, mainly used in Southeast Asian cookery (with lamb, beef or chicken). To be at its best, you need at least two hours marinading time for this one, before cooking. But it will taste good, even without that!

For the rest:

* 450g chicken breast
* 200ml unsweetened coconut milk
* 1 tbsp soft light brown sugar
* 2 tbsp fish sauce
* 1 tbsp ground coriander
* 1 tsp cumin
* ½ tsp turmeric
* 1 lemongrass stalk

## What to do

**1** Soak some wooden skewers in water for 1 hour.

Now prepare the chicken...

**2** Slice the chicken into thin strips.

**3** Remove the tough outer layer of the lemongrass, top and tail it and chop the remaining stalk finely. Combine the coconut milk, brown sugar, fish sauce, coriander, cumin, turmeric and lemongrass in a large bowl. Stir in the chicken and refrigerate for 2 hours, or overnight if possible.

Next the dip...

**4** Place the peanuts in a food processor and whiz until finely ground. Set aside.

**5** Discard the tough outer skin from the lemongrass and top and tail, finely chop the rest of the lemongrass and put in the food processor along with the shallot, garlic, ginger, turmeric and sunflower oil. Whiz until it's a smooth paste.

**6** Over a low heat, gently cook the paste for 5 minutes, stirring regularly until softened. Stir in the peanuts, sugar, fish sauce and chilli sauce, lime, water and coconut milk and cook for 10 minutes, stirring occasionally. The sauce needs to thicken slightly. Transfer to a bowl, ready to serve.

**7** Finally, preheat the grill. Skewer a piece of chicken on each stick and grill for 4 minutes on each side, or until the chicken is cooked through. Then get dipping!

**83**

# Traditional English tea

## (scones, jam and clotted cream with a pot of tea) (v)

Call it heaven on a plate if you like, but, although it originated in Devon and Cornwall, you're more likely to be served a cream tea in New York than in London, because New Yorkers think they're quaint.

For the scones:

* ✱ 225g plain flour
* ✱ 1 tsp cream of tartar
* ✱ 1 tsp bicarbonate of soda
* ✱ 25g butter
* ✱ 150ml buttermilk
* ✱ strawberry jam
* ✱ clotted cream
* ✱ butter

You can get this in most supermarkets. Otherwise, add a bit of lemon juice to fresh milk for a similar taste.

For the pot of tea:

* ✱ 6 teabags
* ✱ milk
* ✱ sugar (if you like it)

Or 6 tsp of tea leaves. After all, this is a traditional tea.

It's not the British way to serve butter on the scones as well as cream and jam (too indulgent) but I always add butter to mine...

HOW TO MAKE A CUP OF TEA

## What to do

For the scones:

**1** Sift the flour with the bicarbonate of soda and cream of tartar into a mixing bowl. Then rub in the butter. Make a well in the centre of the flour and pour in the buttermilk, mixing quickly to a soft dough.

> It's disappointing to eat the scones cold. Get it right, serve them toasty.

**2** Turn the dough onto a floured board and knead lightly until smooth. Roll out until it's just less than 2 cm thick. Stamp out into 12 rounds with a 5 cm pastry cutter. Leave to stand for 15 minutes. Put the rounds on a heated greased baking sheet and bake for about 10 minutes or until the scones are well-risen and golden.
Transfer to a wire rack and cool slightly (but only slightly).

For the tea:

Fill the kettle with 8 cups of water and boil. Place the teabags, or tea leaves in the teapot and fill with boiled water. Serve with milk in a jug and a bowl of sugar.

> My mum always says, 'Warm the teapot first'. This means swirling the teapot with hot water, then emptying it. Then, put in the tea, pour on the boiling water and let it brew for 5 minutes. If using leaves, you will need a strainer to pour the tea through.

# Profiteroles
## with hot chocolate sauce (v)

**serves 4**

For the choux pastry:

* ✳ 150ml water
* ✳ pinch of salt
* ✳ 2 free-range eggs
* ✳ 50g butter
* ✳ 65g flour

That's the really light pastry you get in eclairs, and... profiteroles.

Like eclairs, but small and round and served with hot chocolate sauce!

For the chocolate sauce:

* ✳ 200g dark chocolate
* ✳ 125ml double cream

For the filling:

* ✳ 150ml fresh double cream
* ✳ 1 tbsp caster sugar

### What to do

**1** Preheat the oven to 200°C.

**2** To prepare the pastry, sift the flour and salt onto a large square piece of greaseproof paper and set aside.

**3** Put the water, butter and salt in a saucepan and heat gently until the butter has melted. Bring slowly to the boil and, just before boiling point, remove the pan from the heat and quickly pour the flour into the pan, and beat in the flour all at once with a wooden spoon. Place back on a low heat and stir until the mixture draws away from the sides of the pan and forms a ball. Don't overbeat or the mixture will become fatty. Leave to cool slightly. Beat in the eggs gradually, with a hand whisk or an electric whisk, until the pastry is smooth and glossy.

**4** The mixture will be shiny and smooth and will fall reluctantly from a spoon if it is given a sharp jerk.

5 Line a baking tray with greaseproof paper. Dip a teaspoon into warm water and spoon out a teaspoon of the mixture. Rub the top of the mixture with a wet finger and, using another spoon, put onto the baking tray. This ensures a crisper topping. Bake just above the centre of the oven for 25–30 minutes or until the pastry is well-risen and crisp.

6 Remove from the oven and make a slit in the base of the profiteroles. This lets the steam out, so they don't go soggy. Leave to cool on a wire rack.

7 Whisk the cream and sugar together until thick.

8 Place the chocolate and double cream into a small saucepan and heat gently, stirring until the chocolate has melted and the sauce has thickened. Remove from the heat and cool slightly.

9 To fill the profiteroles, cut in half and place a spoonful of cream in the middle. Then put the two halves together.

10 Pile the profiteroles in a bowl and serve with the sauce poured over.

One of my favourite sauces, (which is fantastic on vanilla ice cream and just might work on a profiterole, is melted Mars bar. Just cut the bar into little pieces and melt slowly with a little milk. Poured straight onto ice cream, it hardens and, hey presto, you've got a toffee and chocolate sauce. But don't say I told you... Instead, pretend you hand-picked the toffees and ground the cocoa beans yourself.

# Glittery cupcakes (v)

Good looks are half the battle with party food. These are really pretty.

- ✻ 185g self-raising flour
- ✻ 1 tsp baking powder
- ✻ 185g caster sugar
- ✻ 185g butter, softened
- ✻ 1 tsp vanilla extract
- ✻ 3 free-range eggs, lightly beaten
- ✻ 250g royal icing sugar
- ✻ 1 tbsp water
- ✻ edible glitter

You can buy this from specialist cake shops.

You could add a smartie or crystallised fruit on top. Or a raspberry, or anything you fancy really!

SUGAR

BUTTER

**What to do**

1 Preheat the oven to 180°C and line a muffin tray with paper muffin cases.

2 Sift the flour, baking powder and a pinch of salt into a large bowl. In a separate bowl, whisk the sugar, butter and vanilla extract with an electric whisk until light and fluffy. Gradually whisk in the eggs, then gradually add the flour.

3 Fill each paper case in the tray with a large tablespoon of mixture. Place the tray in the preheated oven and bake for 12–15 minutes or until slightly golden on top. Remove the cupcakes from the tray and leave to cool on a wire rack.

For the icing:

**4** Put the icing sugar in a bowl and drop small amounts of the water into it. Mix in until the icing is thick but glossy.

You need less water than you think, so just add tiny bits at a time.

**5** Using a teaspoon, spoon the icing onto the cakes and swirl around to cover.

**6** Sprinkle on the glitter and serve.

You can use drops of food colouring to make the icing different colours. You only need to use a tiny bit, unless you're doing Halloween cakes for little kids, in which case gruesome reds and glaring greens are fine.

We need more cupcakes on the left

Balanced Diet

serves 6 to 8

# BBQ Lamb in pitta pockets

## with homemade hummus

For the homemade hummus:

* 3 cloves of garlic, chopped
* 4 lemons, juice only
* 1 tin of chickpeas, washed and drained
* 50g tahini
* 3 tbsp extra-virgin olive oil
* salt and black pepper

You can find this in the herb and spice section.

For the rest:

* 1.8kg butterflied leg of lamb
* 1 tsp sea salt
* 2 tbsp extra-virgin olive oil
* 2 cloves of garlic, crushed
* 2 sprigs of rosemary, chopped finely
* black pepper
* 2 tbsp honey
* 12 pitta breads

'Butterflied' means opened out to reduce cooking time and to absorb a marinade better. The butcher will do this for you.

## What to do

**1** Place the lamb in a large shallow bowl. Mix the olive oil, garlic, honey, rosemary, salt and black pepper, rub all over the lamb and refrigerate for a minimum of 2 hours, or overnight.

**2** To prepare the hummus simply put all the ingredients in a blender and whiz until smooth.

**3** Heat the BBQ coals (or if it's gas, heat to medium). Remove the lamb from the marinade, allowing as much marinade as possible to drain back into the bowl. Place the lamb into a large square of silver foil and fold the sides up to make a loose parcel.

**4** Cook the lamb on the BBQ for 25 minutes. Remove from the silver foil and cook for 5 minutes on each side. Be very careful with the hot oil. The lamb should be a little pink inside. Rest for 10 minutes, covered. Slice and serve.

**5** Serve the lamb and hummus with lightly toasted pitta breads, split down the sides.

You can also cook the lamb on a grill plate. Cook over high heat for 5 minutes on each side. Reduce heat to medium and cook, covered, for about 25 minutes or until cooked as desired.

CORDON ~~BLEU~~ NOIR

**makes 10**

# BBQ halloumi and cherry tomato skewers (v)

* 250g halloumi cheese, cut into squares
* 20 cherry tomatoes
* 1 tbsp fresh lemon juice
* 1 tbsp olive oil
* 1 tbsp basil, finely chopped
* black pepper

**What to do**

1 Soak ten skewers in water for 2 hours. Place one square of halloumi on the stick, followed by a tomato, followed by another piece of cheese and another tomato. Repeat with each stick until all the cheese has been used

2 Mix the oil, basil and a pinch of pepper together and drizzle over the skewers. Place them on a medium-hot BBQ and cook for a few minutes, turning so that all sides are grilled. Drizzle with lemon and serve.

# BBQ sticky chicken drumsticks

* 8 chicken drumsticks
* 2 tbsp tomato ketchup
* 2 tbsp soy sauce
* 2 tsp clear honey
* 2 tsp sunflower oil

**What to do**

1 Remove the chicken skin from the drumsticks. Slice a few slashes into each side and cook the chicken on a medium-heat BBQ, turning a couple of times.

2 Mix the ketchup, honey, sunflower oil and soy sauce together. Brush the chicken with the mixture and place back on the BBQ for 10 further minutes, or until the chicken is cooked through, with juices running clear when pierced through the thickest part with a skewer.

# Lemon and mustard new potatoes (v)

serves 4

* 800g new potatoes
* 100ml extra-virgin olive oil
* ½ tsp grated lemon zest
* 4 tbsp lemon juice
* 2 tbsp chopped fresh chives
* 1 tbsp Dijon mustard
* ¼ tsp salt
* 4 free-range eggs, hard boiled

## What to do

1 Place the potatoes in a saucepan and add enough boiling water to just cover them, add some salt and bring them to the boil. Simmer for 20 minutes over a medium heat, or until a knife pierces a potato easily. Drain and place in a large bowl.

2 Cut the eggs in quarters. Mix the olive oil, lemon zest, lemon juice, chives, mustard and salt together to make the dressing. Place the eggs on top of the potatoes. Pour over the dressing and gently turn over the potatoes and eggs to mix the dressing through.

New potatoes are also delicious cold, mixed with sour cream, chopped chives and chopped spring onions.

# Greek Salad (v)

* 450g beefsteak tomatoes, in chunks
* 1 red onion, sliced
* 1 cucumber
* 250g feta cheese, cubed
* 5 tbsp extra-virgin olive oil
* 4 tbsp lemon juice
* 20 black olives
* 1 tbsp flat leaf parsley, chopped
* pitta breads

Serve with warmed pitta bread.

**What to do**

1 Cut the cucumber lengthways and then lengthways again to make into quarters. Cut the seeds out down the length and cut the rest into chunks.

2 Place in a bowl with the tomatoes, red onion, feta and olives.

3 Mix together the olive oil, lemon juice, parsley and a little salt and pepper. Pour over the salad and toss with spoons to make sure the salad is coated with the dressing.

# Fruit sticks with a honey and yoghurt dip (v)

* A punnet each of strawberries, raspberries and blueberries
* 200ml Greek yoghurt
* 2 tbsp lavender honey

**What to do**

1 Wash all the fruit and drain. Place a blueberry, strawberry and a raspberry followed by a blueberry and finally a strawberry on each stick. Pile on a plate.

2 Mix together the yoghurt and honey and put it in a bowl next to the sticks and serve.

serves **4**

# Meringue (v)

* **4 large free-range eggs**
* **115g caster sugar**
* **115g icing sugar**
* **2 drops of vanilla flavouring**

Almost everyone likes meringues, but hardly anyone makes them, even though they taste exactly 496 times better than shop-bought ones. If you make your own, people will think you're very clever. Let them think so, although it's easy peasy. The only secret is very low heat.

## What to do

1 Break the eggs into a bowl and, using a spoon, remove the egg yolks (without breaking them) into a large, clean, dry bowl. Set aside and bring to room temperature.

> I find the easiest way to remove egg yolks is by breaking the egg into a saucer and then covering the yolk with an egg cup and draining the white off into a bowl.

2 Preheat the oven to 100°C. Line a large baking sheet with greaseproof paper.

3 Using an electric whisk on a medium speed, beat the egg whites until the mixture is fluffy and sticks up in stiff peaks when you lift the whisk out. Then, on a fast speed, start adding a spoon of sugar at a time with a few seconds of mixing between. The mixture should be thick and glossy when ready. Sift a third of the icing sugar (plus the vanilla flavouring) into the meringue and fold in, as gently as possible. Continue with each third. Don't over mix, the meringue should be soft and smooth.

4 Using two dessert spoons, scoop heaped spoonfuls onto the prepared baking sheet. Bake for around 1½ hours, or until the meringues sound crisp and dry when tapped from below. Leave to cool on a cooling rack.

# Eton Mess (v)

serves 4

Bubble and squeak, spotted dick, cock-a-leekie,
toad in the hole ... just a few great old Brit food
names. Eton Mess is traditionally served at
Eton's June 4th prize-giving picnic. One anecdote
claims the pudding was invented when a Labrador
accidentally sat on a picnic basket in the back of
a car. In which case, maybe a poodle invented
the pavlova. We shall never know....

* 4 meringue nests
* 250g double cream
* 1 tbsp caster sugar
* 1 punnet of raspberries
* 1 punnet of strawberries
* 1 tbsp runny honey

**What to do**

In a large bowl whisk the double cream until it begins to form
soft peaks. Fold in the sugar and honey. Break the meringue
into the cream and add the fruit and fold.

# Summer Pudding (v)

This might include blackcurrants, redcurrants, raspberries or blackberries.

* 750g mixed soft fruits
* 100g caster sugar
* 2 tbsp water
* 150g crustless stale white bread, thick sliced

**What to do**

1 Put the soft fruits in a saucepan with the sugar and water and cook gently for 5 minutes, or until the juices run and the fruits soften.

2 Reserve 2 slices of bread and then cut the rest of the slices into 3 fingers. Using the top of a 900ml pudding basin as a template, cut a disc of bread from one of the reserved bread slices and push into the bottom of the basin.
Line the sides of the pudding basin with the bread, making sure there are no gaps between the slices, pushing them snugly together, reserve two slices for the top.

3 Put the fruit and all but 2 tablespoons of the fruit juice into the bread-lined basin. Cover with the reserved bread slice, tearing and patching where necessary to make sure there's no fruit showing. Put a plate on top and leave in the fridge to chill overnight.

4 To get it the right way up, hold a serving plate upside-down over the top of the dish and turn the basin over. Use the reserved fruit juice to pour over any parts of the bread that have not been coloured.

# How to Impress Your

# Girlfriend/ Boyfriend

My grandmother used to say 'the way to a man's heart is through his stomach'. Just as well she wasn't a surgeon. Now the tables are turned, which doesn't mean that we have to eat upside down but rather that boys are as likely to try to woo girls with a romantic dinner as the other way round.

The main point of this section's dishes is that each one seems like you've made an effort. They may not be aphrodisiacs exactly, but then it's hard to get powdered rhino's horn at the corner shop.

Add some fancy touches. No need to be cheesy about it, but a red candle stuck in a bottle is a great way to hide the fact that you've left your socks on the table. Splash out on red napkins. A single rose, perhaps. Dandelions if your loved one has a sense of humour. A bowl of purple grapes. Music. Make sure your pants are out. Sorry that should be parents. How about serving the sea bass in a basket?

Above all, check what your loved one likes best. Rack of lamb will become rack-of-pain if she/he is veggie.

# Pan-Fried sea bass
## on buttered spring onion mash

**serves 2**

* 300g potatoes, peeled and cut into chunks
* 1 tsp butter
* 2 spring onions, finely chopped
* 30ml milk
* grated nutmeg
* 2 fillets of sea bass

* 1 tbsp butter
* 1 lemon
* 2 cloves of garlic, crushed
* 40g butter
* salt and black pepper

### What to do

1 Cook the potatoes in boiling salted water until tender, about 15–20 minutes, or until the potatoes fall off the knife when pierced. Drain them, add 1 tablespoon butter, and then mash them, also beating in the spring onions, milk, grated nutmeg, salt and pepper.

Why 'pan-fried'? What else would you fry a fish in? A hat? In fact, pan-frying means shallow frying, using only a little oil. And why 'sea'? Where else do fish live? Well in fact the word 'Bass' covers a multitude of fish, and some are found in fresh water.

2 Fry the sea bass fillets, skin-side down, until golden brown in a little olive oil and turn them over, adding a knob of butter and squeeze of lemon juice. Place in a warm dish.

3 Over a low heat, using the same frying pan, add the rest of the butter. When the butter's gently sizzling, add the garlic and fry for a couple of minutes, don't let it brown. Add the rest of the lemon juice and heat through. Season with a little salt and pepper.

4 Serve by placing the mash in the centre of the plate, lean the sea bass on the potato (skin side down) and drizzle a little of the lemony butter sauce over the fish.

# Baked Italian pork cutlets

* 2 pork cutlets
* 1 tbsp olive oil
* 1 clove garlic, finely chopped
* 2 tsp fresh oregano, chopped
* 2 tsp fresh rosemary, chopped
* 1 tbsp balsamic vinegar
* 1 large tomato, roughly chopped
* 1 pepper (red or yellow), cut in half with seeds removed
* salt and black pepper

**What to do**

1 Preheat the oven to 220°C.

2 Place the pepper on a baking tray under a hot grill, skin side up. Grill for 10 minutes, or until the skin is blistered and blackened. When cooled, peel off the skin and slice into strips.

3 Combine the oil, garlic, oregano, rosemary, balsamic vinegar and a pinch of salt and pepper in a bowl. Add the cutlets to the bowl and cover them with the sauce. Refrigerate for 30 minutes.

4 Place the cutlets in a single layer on a baking sheet and bake for 15 minutes. Place the peppers and tomatoes on top of them and gently pour over the rest of the sauce, bake for a further 15 minutes.

Delicious served with creamy mustard mash (see page 24). Add mustard to the mash to spice it up!

serves
**②**

# Sautéed chicken fillets

## with lemon and parsley butter

Sautéeing is a little like pan-frying, only using a higher heat.

* 1 tbsp vegetable oil
* 5 tbsp butter
* 2 whole chicken breasts
* 1 lemon, juiced
* 3 tbsp chopped fresh parsley
* salt and freshly ground pepper

**What to do**

1 Heat the oil and 3 tablespoons of the butter in a frying pan over medium-high heat. When the butter foam begins to subside, sauté the chicken fillets on both sides, making sure the chicken is cooked through (no pink bits). Then remove the fillets to a warm plate and add salt and pepper.

2 Add the lemon juice to the pan and turn on the heat to medium. Add up to a couple of tablespoons of water if needed. Add the parsley and the remaining 2 tablespoons butter to the cooking juices and stir several times.

3 Lower the heat to very low and add the cooked chicken fillets, turning them over quickly in the sauce once or twice.

**4** Transfer the fillets to a warm serving dish and pour the cooking juices from the skillet over them. Serve with any kind of potatoes and some lovely fresh green French beans! If you use frozen green beans, only boil them for about five seconds. Otherwise they go mushy.

He made you a Valentine meal of sauteed chicken?

Correct

So why did you dump him?

I'm vegetarian

# Herb encrusted rack of Lamb

**serves 2**

* 1 rack of lamb, 8 bones, French trimmed
* 1 tbsp Dijon mustard
* 1 tsp thyme, chopped
* 2 tsp rosemary, chopped
* 2 cloves garlic, crushed
* 50g breadcrumbs
* 2 tbsp olive oil
* salt and pepper, to taste

> The butcher can do this for you.

## What to do

1 Preheat the oven to 230°C.

2 Season the lamb all over with salt and pepper. Heat 2 tablespoons olive oil in a large frying pan over high heat. Sear the lamb for 1-2 minutes on all sides. Set aside for a few minutes and let the seared rack of lamb sit for a while until it's cold enough to handle, then brush it with the mustard.

3 Mix the breadcrumbs with the herbs and garlic on a plate and press the rack of lamb in the herb mixture to encrust it completely. Cover the ends of the bones with silver foil, and place the rack of lamb in a baking tray. Then cook in the oven for 20 minutes.

4 Carve the rack between the ribs in portions of 2–3 ribs.

# Lemon and chilli linguine (v)

* 75ml olive oil
* 2 cloves garlic, peeled
* 2 handfuls of rocket
* 2 red chillies, deseeded and finely chopped
* 75g block of Parmesan
* 1 lemon, juiced
* salt and freshly ground pepper
* 300g linguine

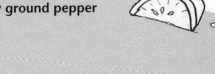

## What to do

**1** Bring a pan of water to the boil in a large saucepan and cook the linguine as per the instructions on the packet. Drain well.

**2** While the pasta's cooking, heat the oil in a pan and gently fry the chillies and garlic for 1–2 minutes. Remove from heat, add the lemon juice and season with salt and freshly ground pepper.

**3** To serve, place the linguine into a serving dish, pour over the oil. Toss in the rocket and shave some Parmesan over the top.

> Linguine is like flat spaghetti, which you can always use instead if you like, since it's more likely to be in your cupboard.

serves 2

# Herby fishcakes
## with homemade aioli

For the fishcakes:

* **400g potatoes**
* **400g fish, skinned and filleted**
* **200g fresh brown breadcrumbs**
* **1 free-range egg**
* **1 lemon, zest only**
* **1 tbsp parsley, chopped**
* **½ tbsp dill, chopped**
* **1 tbsp plain flour**
* **salt and freshly ground black pepper**
* **1 tsp milk**

You could use salmon, cod or haddock.

For the aioli:

* **3 large egg yolks**
* **3 cloves garlic**
* **½ lemon, juice only**
* **200ml extra virgin olive oil**
* **2 tsp Dijon mustard**
* **salt and black pepper**

Aioli is a delicious mayonnaise-like sauce traditionally served with chunks of fresh bread but lovely with a selection of fresh raw vegetables, such as celery, carrot or cucumber sticks.

### What to do

To cook the fishcakes...

**1** Put the fillets of fish into a large frying pan and pour in just enough cold water to cover them. Over a medium heat, gently bring the water to the boil. Cover the pan and simmer gently for about 5 minutes, reducing the heat if necessary. Drain the fish and transfer to a plate. Allow the fish to cool.

**2** Bring a large pan of salted water to the boil and in the meantime wash, peel and quarter the potatoes. Place the potatoes into the boiling water and cook until they are soft (about 15 minutes). Drain the potatoes and mash with a potato masher, until they're smooth and lump-free. Set aside.

**3** Flake the fish with a fork, making sure there are no bones. Then, in a mixing bowl, combine the fish, potatoes, lemon zest, parsley, dill, milk and seasoning to taste. Bind the mixture.

**4** Prepare three separate bowls and fill one with the flour, one with the beaten egg and the last one with the breadcrumbs. On a floured board, break the mixture into four equal pieces and shape the mixture into four balls, gently pressing each ball down to make a cake shape. Dip the cakes first into the flour, then the beaten egg, then into the breadcrumbs ensuring that they're evenly coated. Chill on a plate in the fridge until needed.

**5** When ready, heat the oil in a medium-sized pan and add the fishcakes, gently frying each side for about 5 minutes or until the breadcrumbs are golden and the cakes are thoroughly heated through.

Try serving the fishcakes with a fresh green salad.

And now prepare the aioli...

**6** Whizz everything except the olive oil in a food processor. When combined, pour the oil very slowly through the funnel into the processor in a thin stream. The mixture should be a smooth, thick, vibrant yellow sauce. To vary the flavour, add a little mustard or some saffron.

serves
②

# Roasted tomato, mozzarella and spinach gnocchi (v)

* 300g large ripe tomatoes, halved
* ½ onion, sliced
* 1 clove garlic, finely sliced
* ½ tsp oregano
* ½ tsp brown sugar
* ½ tsp balsamic vinegar
* 1 tbsp olive oil

* 200g spinach
* freshly ground nutmeg
* 200g gnocchi
* 150g mozzarella, cubed
* basil leaves
* 20g Parmesan
* salt and black pepper

**What to do**

1 Preheat the oven to 190°C.

2 Mix the onions, garlic and oregano and use them to cover the base of an oiled baking tray. Layer the tomatoes, cut-side up. Season with salt and pepper and sprinkle with the sugar, vinegar and 1 tablespoon olive oil and roast for 1 hour. When ready, the tomatoes should have shrunk and the onions should be soft and brown. Cook for 10 more minutes if necessary. Allow to cool and then whizz in a food processor.

For the gnocchi:

**1** Pre-heat the oven to 200°C.

**2** Rinse the spinach and place it in a saucepan, wilt over a medium heat. Drain the spinach and, when cool, squeeze out as much of the excess liquid as possible.

**3** Cook gnocchi according to instructions. Spread the spinach over the base of a baking tray, season with salt and pepper and nutmeg, and spread the cooked gnocchi over the spinach, then pour over the tomato sauce. Scatter mozzarella and basil on top and push gently down into the gnocchi. Grate over the Parmesan and drizzle with the rest of the olive oil.

**4** Bake for 20–25 minutes until bubbling, and combine with the roasted vegetables.

spinach before cooking

Spinach after cooking.

GREAT CULINARY QUESTIONS (No 89)

Why does spinach shrink?

# Onion and sundried tomato fougasse (v)

* 450g strong white flour
* 7g fast-action yeast
* ½ tsp salt
* 300ml water
* 6 tbsp olive oil
* ½ onion, finely chopped
* 4 sundried tomatoes, finely chopped
* ½ tsp sea salt
* 1 tsp oregano

> This is nice flat bread, which you might also know as 'share and tear'. It's good to have in the middle of the table so that you can just pull pieces off.

**What to do**

1 Mix 200g of the flour with all of the yeast and about 150ml water in a bowl. Beat together into a thick batter for 3 minutes. Leave to rise in a warm place, in a clean bowl covered with cling film (an airing cupboard works well) to make a sponge-like mixture – this should happen in 1½ hours. Then add the rest of the flour, salt, water and 2 tablespoon of oil, and mix well.

2 Turn out onto a lightly floured work surface and knead to a smooth dough for about 5 minutes. Put the dough back in the bowl to rise, covered with cling film, for a further 1 hour until doubled in size.

> For how to knead see page 135.

3  Fry the onions in 1 tablespoon of oil and leave to cool.

4  Knock the risen dough back and knead in the onions and sundried tomatoes to the dough until well mixed in. Divide into 3 pieces and, using a rolling pin, roll out each piece to about 2.5 cm high, shape into a circle.

5  Place the circles on baking sheets, lined with baking parchment (a non-stick paper that doesn't need greasing). Using a sharp knife, slash through the dough, one slash in the middle at the top and three slashes down each side to form the impression of a leaf. Brush with 2 tablespoons of oil and sprinkle with the sea salt and oregano and leave for a further hour, until doubled in size.

6  Heat oven to 230°C and bake the loaves for 15 minutes, until golden brown. Brush with the remaining oil as the loaves cool on a wire rack.

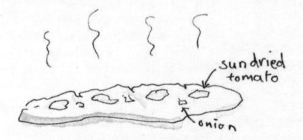

It wasn't so long ago that the British didn't know what a baguette was. Now we know Panini, chapatti, bagel, nan and, yes, fougasse!

# Caramelised red onion and goat's cheese tart (v)

* 2 red onions, sliced
* 1 tbsp olive oil
* 1 tbsp red wine vinegar
* 1 tsp fresh thyme, chopped
* 1 tbsp sugar
* 1 goat's cheese
* 1 tbsp pine nuts
* 1 free-range egg, lightly beaten
* 1 block of puff pastry

**What to do**

1 Over a medium heat, cook the onions in the olive oil and keep stirring so the onions don't catch and brown. When the onions are nicely cooked, add the vinegar and sugar and cook until the vinegar has simmered down to a syrup. Add the thyme and cook over a low heat for another 5 minutes.

2 On a floured surface, roll out the puff pastry to 3 cm thick and cut out 2 circles (using a side plate as a template). Place on greaseproof paper on a baking sheet.

**3** Brush around the outside of the pastry disks with the egg, place the onions in the middle and spread out to cover the pastry, leaving a 2.5 cm edge.

**4** Cut discs of the goat's cheese and place over the onion, sprinkle any crumbly bits over the top, then sprinkle the pine nuts over the top.

**5** Bake for 15 minutes or until the pastry is cooked underneath and is golden brown.

Serve with a rocket and cherry tomato salad.

Mmmm! Just like nanny used to make

serves **2**

# Juniper cabbage (v)

* ½ white cabbage
* 1 small onion, thinly sliced
* 1 clove garlic, crushed
* 2 juniper berries, crushed
* 1 tsp olive oil

> This should convert all cabbage haters!

## What to do

1 In a medium saucepan, heat the olive oil over a low heat and fry the onion, juniper berries and garlic gently.

2 Take the end of the cabbage off with a sharp knife, remove the outer leaves and thinly slice.

3 When the onion's cooked, add the cabbage so it's coated with the onion and olive oil and continue cooking, with a lid on, for another 10 minutes or until the cabbage is cooked but still has a slight crunch to it.

One of my favourites is red cabbage, cooked as here, but substituting the juniper berries with one chopped apple, a teaspoon of vinegar, a tablespoon of butter and some brown sugar

# Broccoli and cauliflower cheese (v)

serves 2

* 1 whole head of broccoli
* ½ head of cauliflower
* 100g mature Cheddar, grated
* 20g butter
* 20g plain flour
* 300ml milk
* 1 bay leaf
* salt and white pepper
* nutmeg to grate

**What to do**

1 Preheat the oven to 180°C.

2 Butter a large ovenproof dish.

3 Bring a large saucepan of water to the boil, add the broccoli and cauliflower and cook for 3 minutes. Drain thoroughly.

> Nice variation on traditional cauliflower cheese, but leave out the broccoli (or the cauliflower!) if you like. Comforting on a cold winter evening....

4 Make the béchamel sauce as on page 28. Add 100g of the cheese and stir until melted.

5 Lay the vegetables in the prepared dish and pour over the cheesy sauce. Grate a little nutmeg over the top and then sprinkle with the rest of the cheese and bake for 20 minutes or until the top is golden and bubbling.

This is lovely with the oven baked butterflied leg of lamb or as a stand-alone dish.

> Skip the nutmeg if you're not a fan!

# makes 12 Italian chocolate mousse (v)

Really this should be called French Chocolate mousse, since mousse is the French word for foam and apparently Louis XVth enjoyed chocolate foam made just like this back in the 18th century.

* **60g of really good chocolate**
* **2 free-range eggs, separated**
* **30g butter**
* **15g sugar**

**1** Melt the chocolate and the butter in a bowl which can sit over a pan of gently simmering water (the water should not be touching the bottom of the bowl), always stirring with a wooden spoon (and don't get any water in the chocolate). Once melted, remove from the heat and add the sugar and the egg yolks. Continue stirring for 5 minutes. Set aside, still keeping the chocolate above the warm water but not on the heat.

I like to use dark chocolate, but any variety works well.

**2** Meanwhile, take the egg whites and whip them with an electric whisk until you have stiff peaks. Extremely gently, with a large spatula, fold the chocolate into the egg whites. Place spoonfuls of the mousse in small bowls or cups and refrigerate for at least 3–4 hours until the mousse is firm.

Put a sprig of mint on top if you've got some handy and serve with the chocolate-dipped shortbread (see opposite) if you're feeling indulgent!

# chocolate-dipped shortbread (v)

makes 12

* 480g plain flour
* pinch of salt
* 25g ground rice
* 50g caster sugar
* 100g butter, chilled
* 1 tbsp caster sugar, for dusting

1 Sift the flour, salt and ground rice into a mixing bowl and stir in the sugar. Add the butter in one piece and gradually rub it into the dry ingredients. Knead until well mixed, do not allow the dough to become sticky. Wrap the dough in cling-film and chill for 30 minutes in the fridge.

2 Roll out the chilled dough on a floured surface to about 4 cm thick and, using a heart cutter, cut out as many biscuits as possible. Chill for a further 15 minutes.

3 Bake the biscuits in the centre of the oven for 30 minutes or until pale golden in colour. Remove from the oven and allow to cool on a wire rack.

4 Line a tray with greaseproof paper and set aside.

5 Melt the chocolate in a bowl over some simmering water (making sure the water doesn't touch the bottom of the bowl) and, when melted, dip one side of the biscuit in. Lay the biscuits on the lined baking sheet and allow to set.

# cheesecake (v)

serves 6 to 8

* 300g digestive biscuits
* 60g unsalted butter
* 225g caster sugar
* 3 tbsp cornflour
* 650g full fat soft cream cheese
* 1 tsp vanilla extract
* 300ml whipping cream
* 2 free-range eggs

**What to do**

1 Preheat the oven to 180°C.

2 Line the outside of the cake tin with tin foil to avoid any of the mixture leaking out as it is cooking.

3 Whiz the biscuits until you are left with fine crumbs. Or, you can just crumble the biscuits in your hands or bash them with a rolling pin. This helps in the fight against global warming by saving on both electricity and washing up.

4 Melt the butter and mix with the biscuit crumbs in a bowl.

5 Line the bottom of the cake tin with the biscuit mixture.

6 Whiz the sugar, cornflour and cream cheese until the mixure is smooth.

**7** Add the eggs and vanilla and whiz again.

**8** Whilst blending the mixture, add the cream gradually. This should leave a thick, creamy consistency.

**9** Pour this mixture into the cake tin, on top of the biscuit layer.

**10** Place the tin inside a deep baking dish, and add boiling water to the dish, so that it reaches half way up the side of the cake tin.

**11** Put the dish in the oven and bake for 40–50 minutes.

**12** Allow to cool and the put in the fridge overnight.

> When the cheesecake is ready it should be golden, but still a bit wobbly in the middle.

Now for the topping! Jamie Oliver likes his cheesecake with a fruit compote (fruit in a sugary syrup), Delia Smith adds nuts and creme fraiche , Gordon Ramsay has been known to cover his with Mandarin slices, Nigella Lawson dusts hers with icing sugar and berries. I recommend Maltesers.

# makes 12 Honey, cherry and almond granola bars (v)

* 115g honey
* 55g butter, melted
* 3 free-range egg whites
* 1 teaspoon allspice
* ½ tsp almond essence
* 250g granola, either bought or made
* 40g almonds, coarsely chopped
* 85g dried cherries

Use the granola recipe on page 46, or buy it if you don't have the time.

## What to do

1 Preheat the oven to 170°C.

2 Whisk together honey, melted butter, allspice, egg whites, and almond essence. Stir in the granola, almonds and cherries.

3 Pat the mixture into a non-stick (or well-greased) square pan. Using a piece of wax paper, firmly press the granola mixture in a pan. Bake for 20–25 minutes or until lightly browned. Place the pan on a cooling rack. Cool completely and then cut into bars.

# Snacks and Treats

Ever looked at the ingredients in an average bag of snacks? In the good old days (about 1853) crisps were just potatoes sliced wafer thin and sizzled in oil. Now, they'll still be about a quarter potato and the rest will be sugar, dried whey, salt, Acidity Regulator:Sodium Diacetate, Flavour Enhancer:Monosodium Glutamate, high fructose corn syrup, Citric Acid, gluten, soy, strychnine, arsenic (OK, I added those two just to check you're concentrating) etc etc. On the pack there'll be something jazzy like '30% less salt!'. Ask yourself: 'less salt than what?'

So at least learn how to make your own sweet and spicy nuts, cookies, muffins and dips and get three benefits rolled up in one: Health, wealth and a nice smug glow.

Snack tip: Don't put saucers of snacks near ash trays. A friend of mine, approaching the boy-of-her dreams, grabbed a handful of cashews which turned out to be dogends.

# Marinated olives (v)

Dried herbs are fine if you can't get fresh.

* 250g black olives
* 250g green olives
* 5 tbsp extra virgin oil
* 1 tbsp each of rosemary and oregano, finely chopped
* 1 large clove of garlic, sliced thinly
* 1 tbsp red wine vinegar
* 150g feta cheese, cubed
* lemon slices, quartered

**What to do**

1 Mix all the ingredients except the feta cheese together.

2 Add the feta and mix in gently.

3 Cover and set aside for 2 hours before serving.

PITTED OLIVES ←This means the stones are removed

# Sweet and spicy nuts

serves **4**

* 150g unsalted mixed nuts such as pecans and whole almonds or walnuts
* 1½ tbsp unsalted butter
* 2 tbsp firmly packed soft brown sugar
* 1½ tbsp granulated sugar
* ½ tsp paprika
* ½ tsp cayenne
* 1 tsp flaked sea salt

**What to do**

1 Preheat the oven to 180°C.

2 Melt the butter in a large heavy bottomed pan over a medium heat. Add the nuts and sauté, stirring, until lightly browned, for 3–4 minutes. Stir in the brown sugar and continue to stir, until lightly caramelised. Stir in the paprika, cayenne and salt.

3 Transfer the nuts to a sheet of foil, spread out and cool.

This recipe makes 2 bowls of delicious snacks. It's always a good idea to make more, because it's almost impossible not to nibble half before sharing.

serves 4

# Guacamole
## with tortilla chips (v)

* ❋ 2 ripe avocados
* ❋ ¼ onion, finely chopped
* ❋ 1 garlic clove, peeled and finely chopped
* ❋ 1 tomato
* ❋ 1 tbsp spicy tomato salsa
* ❋ lime, 1 tsp juice
* ❋ 1 packet cool tortilla chips

**What to do**

1 Cut the avocados in half, cutting around the stone and twisting the halves apart. With a spoon, lever out the stone. Peel the skin off the avocados or scoop the flesh out with a spoon and place in a medium-sized bowl, add all the other ingredients and mash with a potato masher or a fork until combined.

2 Don't make it too smooth or the guacamole loses its texture.

Serve with a bowl of tortilla chips.

# Blueberry bakewell tart (v)

serves 4

* 375g fresh shortcrust pastry
* 100g melted butter
* 100g caster sugar
* 3 free-range eggs
* 100g ground almonds
* 50g toasted almonds
* blueberry jam
* 125g blueberries, washed and dried

1 Preheat the oven to 190°C.

2 Roll out the pastry and line a loose-bottomed tart tin. Prick the base and line with foil.

3 Bake for 15 minutes at 190°C. Remove the foil and return to the oven for 5 minutes until the pastry's a pale biscuit colour.

4 Melt the butter and sugar in a pan, pour into a bowl and beat in the eggs and almonds.

5 Spread the tart case with a little jam and the blueberries, then pour the egg mixture carefully over the top. Bake in the oven for 20 minutes until the mixture is golden, risen and springy to the touch.

# makes 16 chocolate chip and raisin oatmeal cookies (v)

* 85g unsalted butter, at room temperature
* 115g light muscovado sugar
* 1 free-range egg, beaten
* 115g self-raising flour
* 55g oatmeal
* ¼ tsp cinnamon
* 80g raisins
* 80g chocolate chips

**What to do**

1 Preheat the oven to 180°C.

2 Beat the butter and sugar together until pale and fluffy, in a large bowl, then gradually beat in the egg.

3 Measure the flour and cinnamon into a small bowl and then sift into the large bowl.

4 Fold in the oatmeal, raisins and chocolate chips.

**5** Grease 2 large baking sheets with a little butter, rubbing it all over. Place heaped teaspoonfuls of the cookie mixture onto the baking sheets, leaving enough space around each cookie to allow it to spread during baking.

**6** Bake for 10–12 minutes, or until golden brown. Cool slightly on the baking sheets, then transfer to a wire rack and leave to cool.

These cookies can be kept in an airtight container for 3–4 days.

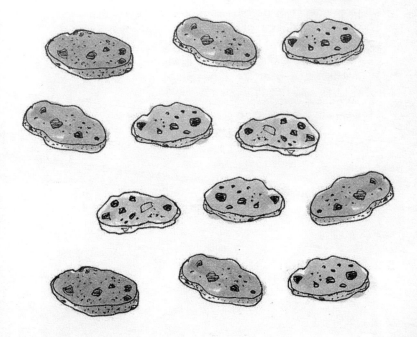

serves
**6**

# Simple apple cake (v)

* 1 tsp cinnamon
* 190g self-raising flour
* 170g unsalted butter
* 100g caster sugar
* 3 free-range eggs
* 2 tbsp milk
* 2–3 eating apples, peeled, cored and thinly sliced

## What to do

1 Preheat the oven to 170°C.

2 Sift the cinnamon and flour together into a bowl.

3 In another large bowl, cream the butter and sugar together until soft and light. Beat in 1 of the eggs, then add 1 tablespoon of the flour and beat in another egg. Add another egg and another tablespoon of flour. Fold in another three-quarters of the remaining flour. Then stir in the milk and fold in the last of the flour.

4 Grease a large roasting pan (or oven dish), then cut greaseproof paper to fit the bottom and sides of the pan and line them with the paper.

**5** Pour half the batter into the pan and level off with a spatula. Layer the apple slices over it and cover with the rest of the mixture.

**6** Bake for 40–45 minutes, until golden brown and, when pierced in the middle, the skewer comes out clean, with no wet mixture attached. Turn out onto a cooling rack and leave to cool.

# makes 12 chocolate truffles (v)

* 150g double cream
* 10g golden syrup
* 300g dark chocolate, at least 50% cocoa solids, broken into small pieces
* 10g unsalted butter
* 150g mixed nuts
* 30g of cocoa powder

**What to do**

1 Over a low heat, mix together the cream and syrup and bring it to boil in a small saucepan. When bubbles start to rise, pour the mixture over 200g of the chocolate and let it sit for about 60 seconds, to allow the chocolate to melt. Then whisk until the mixture's smooth.

2 Pour the chocolate mixture into a shallow container and level off with a spatula. Refrigerate for 2 hours, until the mixture is firm enough to roll with your hands.

3 Melt the remaining 100g of dark chocolate using the microwave – it should take about 40 seconds. Take care not to over-heat the chocolate, as it goes grainy. If it needs a little more time, then stir and heat for another 10 seconds and stir again.

**4** Wash your hands in cold water and dry thoroughly, this will stop the chocolate melting when you roll it. Remove the ganache (chocolate mixture) from the fridge and scoop out one heaped teaspoon. Roll it quickly into a ball between your palms. Pierce each ball with a skewer and dip each ball into the melted chocolate and then roll in the nuts, if you are using them. If you're not using nuts then roll the coated truffle ball in the cocoa powder.

**5** Place them on a plate and put them in the fridge until set. Cover with clingfilm and eat within 5 days.

"Carefully prepared chocolate is as healthful a food as it is pleasant; that it is nourishing and easily digested; that it does not cause the same harmful effects to feminine beauty which are blamed on coffee, but is on the contrary a remedy for them"

JEAN-ANTHELEME BRILLANT. SAVAT 1755-1826

# makes 12 Strawberry and cream muffins (v)

* 2 free-range eggs
* 1 tsp vanilla extract
* 280ml single cream
* 220g sugar
* 400g plain flour
* 3 tsp baking powder
* ¼ tsp salt
* 175g fresh strawberries, chopped

**What to do**

1 Preheat the oven to 190°C.

2 In a large bowl, mix together the eggs, sugar, cream and vanilla.

3 In another large bowl, mix the flour, salt and baking powder together and add the strawberries. Mix so the strawberries are coated in flour. Lightly mix in the cream, but don't over-mix or the muffins won't be as fluffy.

4 Line a muffin tray with muffin cases and fill almost to the top with the mixture.

5 Bake for 20–25 minutes, or until well risen. The muffins are cooked when a skewer is inserted into the middle of one and it comes out clean.

# Fast Food

Same advice as for snacks: handmade is healthier, tastier, better for the environment... I'm not boring you, I hope? Alright, it's not as fast, *exactly*, as a take-away. But all these are pretty quick to make and, really, what do you DO with all that time you're saving by not cooking? Go on. Write it down, I just did. It went like this: Text. Text. Yawn. Text. Stare out of the window wondering about the meaning of life. Text.

Imagine instead you could have been listening to music and knocking up a Perfect Pizza, or a real chicken Korma without a ready-made sauce! On top of which, everyone knows if you get a take-away, first, you've got to find the menu. Then the money. Then ring them up. Give your order. Hang around till it comes. OR go ALL the way to the carry out. In the rain. It's a no-brainer.

makes **3**

# Perfect Pizza (v)

> OK, you can buy pizza shells and just add toppings, but it's impressive to make your own dough. In fact, this may be one of the only things you were taught to make at primary school...

**For the pizza dough:**

* 700g bread flour
* 400ml hand warm water
* 40g sachet of yeast
* 1 tbsp olive oil
* 1 tsp salt
* 1 tsp sugar

**For the topping:**

* mozzarella cheese balls
* anything else you like

**For the passatta:**

* 1 tbsp olive oil
* 1 clove of garlic
* 2 tbsp chopped onions
* 2 tins chopped tomatoes
* 2 tbsp tomato puree
* ½ tsp dried oregano
* 2 tsp chopped fresh basil
* 1 tsp sugar
* salt and pepper

> This is the proper Italian name for the tomato sauce!

## What to do

**1** If you've got a mixer with a dough hook, sift the flour and salt in the mixer, then add water, yeast, sugar and olive oil and mix for 5 minutes. A dough hook does the 'kneading' for you, but if you don't have that kind of mixer, here's how to do it. Just sift the flour and salt into a large mixing bowl and make a well in the centre, mix the yeast into the water and oil and then pour it into the well in the centre of the flour. Use your hands and draw the flour into the liquid and bring it all together until you get a rough dough.

**2** Flour your surface and tip the dough onto it. Knead by placing the heel of the hand into the dough and pushing down and away from you, and then folding the dough back over onto itself. Keep turning the dough and repeating until the dough is soft and springy – this will probably take 10 minutes.

**3** Put into an oiled bowl and cover with a cloth. Allow to rise in a warm place for 1 hour.

**4** Meanwhile, make the pasatta. Sweat the chopped onions and garlic in olive oil until soft but not brown, add the rest of the ingredients and simmer for 1 hour over a low heat, stirring every now and then. Finally, season to taste. If you like a smooth sauce, put it through the blender.

This is why you see guys in pizza parlours slapping the dough about. All very exciting. But basically it just means folding the dough again (this presses out gas and helps the yeast to work).

**5** Most books would tell you to 'punch' or 'knock back' the dough at this point. Really, you should fold it quite gently, then divide into 3, roll out each piece into circles of about 5 mm thick and place onto an oiled baking sheet.

**6** When ready, top the pizza base with the pasatta, leaving a 1.5 cm space around the edge.

**7** Rip the mozzarella balls and dot over the pasatta, then add the rest of the toppings. Drizzle with olive oil and bake for 12 minutes at 220°C until crisp.

You can top pizza with all kinds of things – be imaginative!

# Fish and chips

Buy boneless fish fillets.

* 4 fish fillets such as cod, haddock or plaice
* 7g sachet dried yeast
* 300ml milk
* 75g plain flour
* 75g cornflour
* pinch of cayenne pepper

* ¼ tsp baking powder
* 1 small free-range egg
* 1 bottle of vegetable oil
* 125g of plain flour, seasoned with a little salt and pepper

**What to do**

1 Make the chips as per the recipe on page 26 and keep warm in the oven (50°C).

2 Dissolve the yeast in 3 tablespoons of the milk and leave in a warm place, covered, for 15 minutes. Combine the remaining ingredients, except for the egg white, whisk until smooth and mix in the yeast.

3 Whisk the egg white to stiff peaks and fold gently into the batter.

4 Heat 12 cm of the oil in a deep fat fryer or heavy-bottomed pan over a medium heat.

5 Cut the fillets in half and dip them in the seasoned flour, so the fish is lightly covered. Test the oil heat by putting a drop of the batter into the oil – it should sizzle and start to puff up. Dip the fish into the batter and, using a long slotted spoon, place it in the oil. Fry 2–3 pieces of fish, making sure they aren't touching or on top of each other. Fry until the fish is crispy and golden (3–4 minutes).

**6** Line a bowl with kitchen roll and remove the fish with a slotted spoon. Put the fish straight into the lined bowl, to drain.

**7** Repeat with the rest of the fish, making sure the temperature of the oil is correct.

**8** Keep the fillets of fish warm in the oven with the chips.

**9** Serve as soon as all the fish is cooked with a good dollop of ketchup and a little salt and vinegar if you fancy them.

If you're cooking these for anyone over 40, you could wrap them up in newspaper, because that's how fish'n'chips always used to be served!

I prefer mine wrapped in the Telegraph

# chilli con carne
## on a baked sweet potato

* 1 tbsp vegetable oil
* 1 large onion, peeled and chopped
* 1 red pepper, seeded and chopped into bite-sized pieces

> This is pretty hot and spicy, be warned!

* 2 cloves of garlic, crushed
* 500g minced beef
* 1 tsp chilli powder
* 1 tsp paprika
* 1 tsp ground cumin
* 1 can of chopped tomatoes
* 2 tbsp tomato puree
* 1 small cube of dark chocolate
* salt and black pepper
* 1 can of red kidney beans, drained and rinsed in cold running water
* 4 large sweet potatoes

> Yes, you have read this right!

**What to do**

1 Preheat the oven to 200°C.

2 Wash the potatoes thoroughly and place on a baking tray. Bake for 1 hour, until the flesh inside is soft.

3 Heat the oil over a low heat, in a large pan. Add the onion, garlic and pepper and fry for 3–4 minutes, until the garlic is golden, stirring occasionally. Turn up the heat and add the mince to the pan, and break it up with your spoon or spatula. The mix should sizzle a bit when you add the mince. Keep stirring occasionally for at least 5 minutes, until all the mince is cooked and there are no pink bits.

Make sure you keep the heat hot enough for the meat to fry and become brown, rather than just stew and get watery.

4 Next, stir in the salt, chilli powder, paprika and cumin. Add the tomatoes and tomato puree and stir. Bring to the boil and turn down to a very gentle simmer and cook for 20 minutes, stirring occasionally.

5 After the 20 minutes is up, add the washed beans and the piece of chocolate, bring back to a gentle simmer and cook for a further 10 minutes. Remove from the heat and leave to rest for 10–15 minutes.

6 Remove the potato from the oven and carefully cut half way through lengthways. Gently squeeze open the potato, ladle over a large spoon of chilli and serve.

Great with the Mexican dip or with a dollop of sour cream...

# Handmade burger
## with all the trimmings

* 500g beef steak mince
* 1 red onion
* 2 tbsp Worcestershire sauce
* 1 tsp Dijon mustard
* 1 large free-range egg
* 1 large handful of breadcrumbs
* 1 tbsp chopped fresh parsley
* 4 slices of mature Cheddar
* olive oil, for brushing
* 4 fresh floured baps
* 1 Little Gem lettuce, leaves separated
* 2 ripe tomatoes, sliced
* tomato relish and tomato ketchup
* salt and black pepper

**What to do**

1 Cut half the onion into rings and set aside.

2 Finely chop the rest and put it into a large bowl, add the mince, breadcrumbs, egg, Worcestershire sauce, dijon mustard and parsley. Season with salt and pepper and mix well with your hands. Shape into 4 balls and press down gently to make burgers. Set aside in the fridge for 30 minutes to firm up.

3 Bring a pan to medium heat and brush the burgers with a little oil and cook for 10–12 minutes, turning occasionally. Add the onion rings to the pan and move the burgers around to fit them in. Place a slice of cheese on each burger and cook for a few more minutes. Remove the burgers and carry on cooking the onion for another couple of minutes.

4 Meanwhile, toast the cut side of the rolls under the grill. Place some onion rings, lettuce and tomato onto the base of each bap.

5 Finally, top with a burger, add some relish and ketchup and top with the remaining half of the bap.

serves 2

# Pork and ginger stir-fry

- ✱ 5 tbsp dark soy sauce
- ✱ 1 tbsp sesame oil
- ✱ 1 tbsp Chinese rice wine
- ✱ 2.5cm ginger root
- ✱ 500g pork tenderloin, trimmed of fat
- ✱ 1 red onion, finely sliced
- ✱ 200g baby corn
- ✱ 200g sugar-snap peas
- ✱ handful of beansprouts
- ✱ 300g cooked medium egg noodles, to serve

You could buy stir-fry pork instead.

**What to do**

**1** Thinly slice the pork (unless you've bought stir-fry pork) and place it in a bowl.

**2** Peel and finely chop the ginger and add it to the soy sauce, Chinese rice wine and sesame oil in a bowl and mix it all together. Add the pork to the marinade and add a pinch of black pepper. Mix together.

**3** Heat a wok or a large frying pan over a medium heat. Take the pork out of the marinade with a slotted spoon and cook it in batches until browned all over.

**4** Set the pork aside in a dish and put the vegetables into the wok, pour over the marinade and stir-fry for 4 minutes. Add the pork and stir-fry for 2 minutes. Add the noodles and stir-fry for 2 minutes.

Browning meat fast on a high heat is called 'searing'.

# Sag Aloo (v)

* 4 tbsp vegetable oil
* 1 onion, chopped
* 2.5 cm ginger, finely chopped
* 1 green chilli, deseeded and finely chopped
* 2 cloves of garlic, crushed
* 1 tsp turmeric
* 450g potatoes, peeled and diced into bite-sized pieces
* 300g baby spinach leaves
* ½ tsp salt
* rice, to serve

This is a lovely, mildly spicy Indian veggie curry.

## What to do

1 Heat the oil over a medium heat. Add the onion and cook until soft and translucent. Add the spices and garlic, fry for a few minutes and then add the potatoes and salt. Stir well and cover. Cook for 10 minutes.

2 Add the spinach and stir occasionally, until the spinach is wilted. Cook for 5 minutes. Check that the potatoes are cooked through, cooking for another few minutes if necessary.

3 Prepare the rice, as per the packet instructions, and serve.

# Parmesan chicken nuggets
## with mustard dip

For the nuggets:

* 4 skinless chicken breasts
* 100g flour
* 75g fresh white breadcrumbs
* 55g Parmesan cheese, finely grated
* 2 free-range eggs
* 2 tbsp olive oil
* 1 tbsp butter
* salt and black pepper

For the dip:

* 1 tsp Dijon mustard
* 1 tsp wholegrain mustard
* 125ml sour cream
* 50ml mayonnaise

Your younger sibling probably asks for these if you ever go for a pub lunch. Now's the time to show them the healthy version.

You can buy these, but it's easy to make them using a grater.

**What to do**

1 Put the chicken between 2 large pieces of cling film and, using a rolling pin, gently pound the chicken until it is half as thick. Slice into long finger shapes.

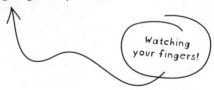

Watching your fingers!

**2** Put the flour into a shallow bowl and add a pinch of salt and pepper. Dip the chicken finger into the flour and shake off the excess.

**3** Lightly whisk the eggs. Mix the Parmesan through the breadcrumbs and dip the chicken fingers into the egg, and then into the breadcrumb mix.

**4** Heat the olive oil and butter in a pan until sizzling hot and fry the fingers for a few minutes on each side until crispy and brown.

**5** For the dip, mix all the dip ingredients together and serve.

Chicken nuggets & chips. Twice

GOURMET CUISINE

# chicken korma

serves 4

* 750g chicken breast, in bite-sized pieces
* 1 tbsp ginger, crushed
* 4 cloves of garlic, chopped
* 1 red chilli, deseeded and finely chopped
* 200g thick plain yogurt
* 2 onions, finely chopped
* 1 tbsp vegetable oil
* 1 tbsp ground coriander
* 1 tsp turmeric
* 1 tsp garam masala
* water
* 75g creamed coconut
* 2 tbsp ground almonds
* 1 tbsp fresh coriander, finely chopped
* ½ lemon, juice only

Fragrant, delicious, very mild curry.

### What to do

1 Place the chicken, garlic and yoghurt into a bowl and mix together, cover and place in the fridge for a minimum of 3 hours or, preferably, overnight to marinate.

2 Using a food processor, whiz the onions and red chillies and blend until smooth. (Add a little water, if necessary.)

**3** In a heavy-bottomed pan, heat the oil over a low heat and add the coriander, turmeric and garam masala. Stir for a minute and add the onion paste from the food processor. Cook for a further 10 minutes.

**4** When the onion is translucent, raise the heat a little, add the chicken and marinated ingredients, and cook, stirring regularly for another 5 minutes. Add the coconut and enough water to cover the chicken. Bring to the boil and stir in the ground almonds. Lower the heat to simmer for a further 30 minutes.

**5** Remove from the heat and add the chopped coriander, lemon, and salt and pepper to taste.

Serve with delicious pilau rice or just plain cooked basmati rice.

No! They're not boil-in-a-bag!

CORN FLAKES

#  Beef chow mein

- ✳ 175g dried medium egg noodles, cooked and drained
- ✳ 1 tsp toasted sesame oil
- ✳ 300g sirloin steak, sliced into strips
- ✳ 6 spring onions, finely chopped
- ✳ 50g mange tout
- ✳ 1 clove of garlic, crushed
- ✳ 1 tbp dark soy sauce
- ✳ 1 tsp fresh ginger
- ✳ 2 tsp rice wine
- ✳ 1 tbsp cornflour
- ✳ 1 tbsp groundnut oil
- ✳ 100g bean sprouts
- ✳ 1 red pepper, deseeded and finely sliced
- ✳ 2 spring onions, sliced lengthways
- ✳ 2 tbsp light soy sauce
- ✳ black pepper

'Mange tout' is French for eat everything

## What to do

1 Drizzle a little sesame oil in the noodles to stop them sticking together when drained.

2 Mix the beef strips in a bowl with the dark soy sauce, honey, rice wine and cornflour and half of the sesame oil, marinade for 30 minutes.

3 Heat the groundnut oil in a wok or deep frying pan until smoking hot and add the beef. Stir-fry for 3 minutes and remove it to a plate.

4 Add the rest of the sesame oil to the pan, then add the red pepper and stir-fry for 1 minute. Add the garlic and ginger, then add the bean sprouts, mange tout and spring onions and stir-fry for 30 seconds. Stir the beef back in and then the cooked noodles and mix in the light soy sauce.

# Egg-fried rice (v)

serves 4

* ✻ 2 tbsp groundnut oil
* ✻ 3 free-range eggs, beaten
* ✻ 300g jasmine rice, cooked according to packet instructions
* ✻ 3 tbsp light soy sauce
* ✻ 1 tsp toasted sesame oil
* ✻ 1 large spring onion, finely sliced

**What to do**

1 Heat a wok or a deep frying pan until smoking hot and add 1 tablespoon of groundnut oil. Add the eggs and mix for a couple of minutes. Remove the eggs to a warm plate and put aside.

2 Reheat the wok and add the remaining groundnut oil. Add the cooked rice and stir well. Fry for 2 minutes.

3 Add the cooked eggs to the wok with the rice, and season, with the soy sauce and sesame oil, to taste. Add in the sliced spring onion and stir.

4 Remove to a warmed bowl.

To cook perfect rice, use about 1½–2 times the amount of water to rice. Place the rice and water in a pan. Heat to boiling, stir once (but only once) then put the lid on the pan and simmer very gently until all the liquid is absorbed. Ideally, you need a pan with a thick bottom and a good tight fitting lid.

# Sweet and sour Vegetables (v)

For the sauce:

* ✳ 3 tbsp brown sugar
* ✳ 1 tbsp rice vinegar
* ✳ ¼ tsp salt
* ✳ 120ml pineapple juice
* ✳ 1 tbsp cornstarch
* ✳ 1 tbsp peanut oil for stir-frying

For the vegetables:

* ✳ 1 onion, sliced
* ✳ 2 medium carrots, sliced
* ✳ 1 large red pepper, deseeded and cut into strips
* ✳ 200g broccoli florets
* ✳ 75g baby corn, halved lengthways
* ✳ 150g beansprouts
* ✳ 90g pineapple chunks

## What to do

1 Mix together all the sauce ingredients in a small bowl.

2 Heat up a wok and add the oil. When the oil is hot, add the vegetables, but keep the pineapple chunks for later. Stir-fry until tender but not overcooked.

3 Give the sauce a quick re-stir then add it to the stir-fry, along with the pineapple chunks. Cook until thickened and steaming hot.

Serve with rice or noodles, whichever you prefer!

serves
4

# Individual chicken and broccoli pies

These are sweet little dishes, which look like you've taken a lot of trouble (but you're buying the pastry ready rolled, so it's not hours of work).

* 60g butter
* 1 leek, peeled and thinly sliced
* 1 cup broccoli, roughly chopped
* 3 chicken breasts, cut into small cubes
* 50g plain flour
* 200ml chicken stock
* 220ml cream
* 1 sheet puff pastry, ready rolled
* salt and black pepper

See page 27 or use a stock cube.

**What to do**

1 Preheat the oven to 180°C.

2 Place the chicken in a covered roasting tin. Cook for 20 minutes.

3 Meanwhile, melt the butter in a saucepan, add the leek and cook for 2–3 minutes. Add the flour and continue to cook until it's bubbling, stirring continuously. Add the stock and bring to the boil, stirring until it thickens. Add most of the cream, keeping back 1 spoonful to glaze the pastry. Over a low heat bring back to a slow boil and then keep on a low heat.

If you have no lid, cover with foil.

**4** When the chicken is cooked, allow it to cool and then chop into small cubes and place into the cream mixture along with the broccoli, and bring back to the boil. Season with a little salt and pepper. Remove from the heat and set aside.

**5** Each individual pie will be cooked and served in a small ovenproof bowl or ramekin. Using the top of the bowls as templates, cut out circles of pastry slightly larger than the bowl being used. Fill each bowl with chicken filling and place the pastry over the top, pressing all the way around to seal. Brush with the remaining cream and cut a slit in the top of the pie to release the steam.

**6** Place on a baking tray and cook for 20–25 minutes until golden.

# Tuna pasta bake

serves **4**

* ✻ 1 small onion, finely chopped
* ✻ 100g frozen peas
* ✻ 100g sweetcorn
* ✻ a squeeze of lemon juice
* ✻ 500ml milk
* ✻ 25g plain flour
* ✻ 2 tins of tuna
* ✻ 1 tbsp olive oil
* ✻ 400g pasta
* ✻ 25g butter
* ✻ 125g Cheddar cheese

**What to do**

**1** Preheat the oven to 160°C.

**2** In a frying pan, stir-fry the onions for 1–2 minutes in a little oil. Drain the tuna well and flake into a bowl.

**3** Cook the pasta in a pan of boiling water as per the instructions on the packet, draining a couple of minutes before the end of the cooking time.

**4** Meanwhile, make the sauce by melting the butter in a saucepan and stirring in the flour. Cook for 1 minute, then gradually stir in the milk to make a thick white sauce. Remove from the heat and stir in all but a handful of the cheese. Turn down the heat to its lowest and let the sauce cook for 2 minutes. Season with a little lemon juice.

**5** Mix the pasta with the frozen peas, sweetcorn, onion, tuna and cheese sauce and pour into an oiled ovenproof baking dish.

**6** Sprinkle with the remaining cheese and cook in the pre-heated oven for about 25 minutes or until the top's golden brown and slightly crunchy.

Free range Pasta drenched in a caramel sauce and served with lashings of sun blush fudge

# Glossary

**Basting** – spooning liquid (such as melted butter) over food while cooking, to prevent the food from drying out

**Bind** – stir an ingredient such as egg into a mixture of food to make it stick together

**Boil** – cook food in boiling liquid (usually water), which means liquid that has reached its highest possible temperature

**Brown off** – cook until brown

**Brush** – rub lightly (a pastry brush can be used)

**Butter (the dish)** – rub a small amount of butter around the inside of the dish you are going to use for cooking, to prevent food sticking to it

**Caramelised** – sugar that is burned till it turns hard

**Carving** – cutting up into pieces

**Crushed** – broken or ground into very small pieces

**Curry paste** – a blend of herbs, spices and seasoning used to make curries, especially Thai ones

**Dry-fry** – fry food without using oil or butter

**Flake** – scraping fish into flakes with a fork

**Fold** – gently blend one ingredient or mixture into another

**Ganache** – mixture of chocolate and cream

**Glaze** – a coating applied to food, such as butter or syrup

**Grated** – broken up into small shreds or fragments by being rubbed against an abrasive surface (usually metal)

**Knead** – mix until smooth (usually dough) by folding, pressing and stretching with the hands

**Knock back dough** – pound the dough to remove any excess air

**Length ways** – in the direction of the length of an object (rather than the width or height)

**Lukewarm** – only slightly warm (not hot)

**Marinade** – liquid mixture, containing herbs and spices, in which food is left to soak for a while to improve the flavour

**Mash** – squash food (such as potatoes or fruit) until it is soft and smooth

**Risen** – dough that has expanded in size so it is no longer flat

**Sauté** – fry food quickly in a frying pan, using a small amount of oil or butter

**Searing** – browning (cooking) meat fast on a high heat

**Simmer** – cook in liquid over a low heat, so that the liquid is almost boiling but not quite

**Softened** – food made less hard, for example butter is kept at room temperature until it is softer than usual

**Stiff peaks** – when a beaten mixture of egg whites or cream reaches a consistency where it is no longer runny but can stand up straight in stiff points

**Stir-fry** – fry food quickly in a small amount of oil over high heat, while stirring continuously

**Taste** – personal opinion (for example, some people may prefer more black pepper in their food to others)

**Top and tail** – trim off the ends of food (such as fruit or vegetables) before cooking

**Well** – hollow made in the middle of a mixture in which another ingredient is placed

**Whisk** – whip food (such as eggs or cream), using a whisk or a fork, until it has a frothy consistency

**Wilted** – food (such as spinach) that has been cooked very briefly until it goes limp

# Index